D0480268

CREATURES
OF THE DEEP BLUE

CREATURES OF THE DEEP BLUE

First published in the United Kingdom by

Evans Mitchell Books
The Old Forge, 16 Church Street
Rickmansworth, Herts WD3 1DH
United Kingdom

Photography and text:
copyright © Jonathan Bird 2008

Jonathan Bird has asserted his rights under
the Copyright, Design and Patents Act 1988
to be identified as the author of this work.

Editing: Peter and Gillian Varley
Design: Darren Westlake
and Julie Cornish at **TU ink**
Pre-press: F E Burman Ltd, London

British Library Cataloguing in Publication
Data. A CIP record of this book is available
on request from the British Library.

ISBN: 978-1-901268-34-8

Printed and bound in Singapore

CREATURES
OF THE DEEP BLUE
JONATHAN BIRD

CONTENTS

INTRODUCTION

I admit it – I have a fabulous job. As a professional underwater cinematographer and photographer, I spend a good deal of time scuba diving in different parts of the world, documenting the creatures I find. It's not particularly glamorous and it doesn't usually pay very well. I sometimes have to spend large blocks of time away from my family, which is the worst part of it. But the good part is that I get to see and do things that most people never will. My films and images bring the world beneath the ocean that I love so much into the lives of others, and that gives me great satisfaction. But the fact is, I do this because I love it and for no other reason. Whether I'm drifting along a colourful Indonesian reef in water as tepid as a bathtub, or fighting my way up current shivering in the icy murk of the north Atlantic,

My friend Glen Holmes who is over 1.8 metres tall and wearing long free-diving fins is dwarfed by a female Sperm whale (*Physeter macrocephalus*) over nine metres long in the waters of Dominica in the Caribbean. The whale stayed with us for over an hour and allowed me to get in and out of the water to change film three times!

I love the thrill of finding interesting subjects to photograph underwater, and watching animals going about their lives in this undersea wilderness.

When I first started out as an underwater photographer, I photographed things in my own backyard – the North Atlantic Ocean off New England. Although we have whales and seals around, the poor visibility and skittish nature of the big stuff meant that most of my photographs featured small animals. It imparted a passion for macro photography – pictures of little things – that exists still. But I longed for interactions with bigger animals like sharks and dolphins. This desire to see and photograph the larger animals of the ocean set me off on diving trips to far away places. For example, while most divers travel to Australia to visit the Great Barrier Reef, I went there to photograph Great White sharks. When I got home – without a tan – and explained to people that I had spent a week in a shark cage immersed in water almost as cold as it is in New England, they thought I was nuts.

Soon I discovered that if one is trying to make a living selling underwater images, sharks sell better than starfish. I began to specialize in photographing big animals, particularly ones that are hard to photograph. I wanted to have images in my library that most other photographers didn't have. I set out on adventures around the world, some successful, but quite a few not so successful, in search of rare and elusive images. The thrill of the hunt becomes intoxicating. There is an immense sense of satisfaction when you have just photographed something that took months

of preparation. It's great when a plan comes together. But not all plans do come together. I have spent many flights home with my head hung low in failure and defeat, thousands of dollars wasted in the pursuit of an image or video sequence that didn't happen. It comes with the territory. My wife Christine is used to cheering me up via e-mail.

Above: In the Turks & Caicos Islands, I had the good fortune to have the correct lens on the camera when a large Humpback whale (*Megaptera novaeangliae*) swam right by me. This shot might appear lucky, but I actually spent seven consecutive days in the water to get the image.

Left: Even a blinding burst of speed will not dislodge the remoras (*Echenseis naucrates*) that cling tenaciously to this Caribbean reef shark (*Carcharhinus perezi*). They get a free meal from the shark's messy eating, and may also benefit the shark by eating parasites, but they annoy the sharks as well.

Sometimes though, just spending a lot of time in the water means I witness things that I couldn't have planned in a million years. I have made discoveries previously unknown to science by pure accident, just by being in the right place at the right time. Sometimes amazing images are the result of pure luck, such as my encounter with an Oarfish in the Bahamas.

In 1996, I spent several days diving with Silky sharks (*Carcharhinus falciformis*) around the AUTEC buoy off New Providence Island, Bahamas. This is a buoy about ten metres across, anchored in over 2,000 metres of water by the U.S. Navy for use in submarine testing at the Tongue of the Ocean off Nassau. When no subs are being tested, the Navy allows diving around the buoy. It is a well-known fact that large floating objects like buoys, logs or sargassum weed often attract large numbers of fish. Frequently, divers at the AUTEC buoy

see not just Silky sharks, but also other pelagic fishes, such as marlin, wahoo and tuna. On the second dive of the day, I jumped off the boat and began a slow descent. When I reached a depth of around 15 metres, I stopped and waited for sharks to swim by. Since the boat captain busied himself with chumming the water above (throwing meat overboard as a lure), I had little trouble finding sharks. Out of the corner of my eye, I saw a shape ascending from the bottomless blue below, about 20 metres away. Swimming as fast as I could, I kept an eye on the shape to determine what it might be. I quickly realized it was a fish, but a species with which I was not familiar. It had an extremely thin, ribbon-like, compressed body which was positioned vertically in the water, with the anterior end pointed up. It had two long 'antennae' with what looked like yellow, diamond-shaped fishing lures on the ends, as well as several along the length of each antenna. It had a large plume of strands on its head, which pointed up towards the surface. The body appeared silvery and reflective. Its dorsal fin ran the length of its back, and undulated to propel the fish. It had no caudal fin, since the body tapered to a point where the tail would be. The large eyes immediately made me think that I was looking at a deep-sea creature.

As I approached within three metres of the fish, I noticed that its antennae were positioned horizontally, one pointing to the left, and the other to the right, so that the animal resembled a cross. I took a shot and noticed that for some reason my strobe didn't fire. (Cameras have a way of failing at a time just like this.) I tinkered

with the strobe cable a bit. As I went to take another shot, the fish began to retreat back into the depths. It first rotated both antennae to vertical, above its head. Then, rather than turn around and swim down head first, the fish undulated its dorsal fin in reverse and swam tail first back into the blue water, quickly going out of sight. It reminded me of a lift, which maintains the same orientation whether it's going up or down. The whole encounter lasted less than 30 seconds.

Of course, when I got back to the dock and described the fish to the people at the dive shop, they thought I was hallucinating. They had never in the past seen such a fish, even though they have dived the exact same site thousands of times. Since I had no idea what I had seen, I contacted Dr. Milton Love, an ichthyologist at the University of California at Santa Barbara, upon my return from the trip. Working from a duplicate slide, he identified

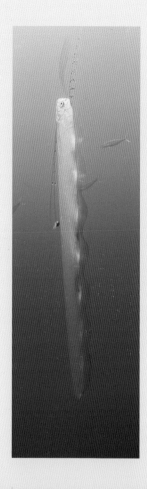

Left: If you stay in the ocean long enough, you see weird things. This is the first Oarfish (*Regalecus glesne*) that was ever photographed alive in its natural habitat.

Far left: In the Galapagos, I kicked hard into the current to get into position for a shot of this magnificent Eagle ray (*Aetobatus narinari*) which was hovering in place over the reef, apparently without any effort. Eagle rays are among the most graceful animals in the ocean.

Below: A mother and calf Bottlenose dolphin (*Tursiops truncatus*) came over to investigate me in the Bahamas. Juvenile dolphins are often more curious than adults, and it seemed at the time that this mother was indulging its baby's curiosity.

Right: A playful Galapagos sea lion (*Zalophus californianus wollebaeki*) smiles briefly before zooming off in the other direction. Sea lions never sit still for long unless they are asleep!

Above: A West Indian manatee (*Trichechus manatus*) grabs a breath from the mirror-like surface in the early morning at Crystal River, Florida.

Right: A Whale shark (*Rhincodon typus*), the largest fish on Earth, opens its mouth to scoop in huge amounts of plankton in the Gulf of Mexico.

Far right: This Green sea turtle (*Chelonia mydas*) woke up just long enough for me to take a picture before it slipped back into a snooze on the reef at Sipadan, Malaysia.

the fish as the Oarfish (*Regalecus glesne*) which reaches 15 metres in length – the longest bony fish on Earth. He passed the image along to Dr. Dick Rosenblatt at Scripps Research Institute, who confirmed the identification, astounded that I was probably the first ever to photograph this animal in its natural habitat. Few of these fish have appeared over the years, usually found dead at the surface or washed up on a beach, so very little is known of their lives or habits.

Several new pieces of scientific information were learned about this fish from my brief encounter. Previously, all the information available came from dead specimens. In observing a living animal, I discovered that the fish swims with undulations of the dorsal fin only, not the entire body. I also found that the Oarfish seems to prefer a vertical orientation in the water column. The way in which it holds its pelvic fins was not known before, and the coloration of the fish (very silvery) was different from that seen in dead specimens.

Sure, I got plenty of shark images on that trip, but I never expected to see something as weird and exciting as an Oarfish. The ocean keeps her secrets well, and it is with great irregularity that we get a glimpse into something new. Who knows what other strange and beautiful animals are lurking below, just waiting to be seen for the first time by mankind? I'm going to keep looking!

This book is a compilation of some of my favourite images of big animals of the ocean and the stories that go with them. I hope it's as interesting to read as it was to photograph, because I had great fun making these images.

SHARKS AND RAYS

Above: The Spotted Eagle ray (*Aetobatus narinari*), with its polka-dotted dorsal surface, soars through the water gracefully, like a giant bird, using its large 'wings' for propulsion.

Left: Reaching four metres and 900 kg, the Tiger shark (*Galeocerdo cuvier*) is one of the larger sharks in the ocean. It is known for a willingness to feed on a wide variety of food and has been blamed for several attacks on surfers in Hawaii.

As I kneeled on the sandy bottom, peering through my viewfinder, I felt a bump on my foot. I looked around and saw I was surrounded by five Tiger sharks ranging in size from two to four metres, not to mention about twenty Lemon sharks. It was noon and I was already on my third tank of the day. We had no cage, no protection, bait all around us, and more sharks than I could possibly hope to keep an eye on at once. For some people this would be a nightmare. For me – heaven. I had travelled to the Bahamas in search of big Tiger sharks and I found them. Lots of them.

Anyone who knows me or looks at my body of work will know that I'm a certified shark nut. Early in my photography career I took a handful of shark images to a calendar publisher and asked them what they thought about a shark calendar. They liked the idea, then looked at my meagre collection of pictures and advised me

The sharks were actually lifting their heads out of the water snapping at me as I was pulled free

A Great white shark (*Carcharodon carcharias*) in South Australia might look like it is attacking the boat, but it's really just holding on to a piece of tuna and won't let go.

to go and shoot a few more. That began a shark quest that has never ended, even though the calendar project only had a lifespan of five years. I am fascinated by sharks, obsessed with finding another interesting species to photograph. I am always interested in the next grand adventure stalking sharks someplace on Earth. Another similarly-minded photographer friend put it well. He said: "Sharks are very dangerous. They eat all my money!"

Given one of my first experiences with sharks, it's actually surprising that I didn't give up. Very early in my shark photography career I was nearly eaten alive by a school of hungry Gray Reef sharks out on Kwajalein Atoll in the Marshall Islands. In 1994, I was there working on my first film about sharks, for a PBS documentary. We chose to work on Kwajalein because the guidebook said that Kwajalein lagoon was 'infested with sharks'. Besides, I had a diving friend who lived there.

For two weeks we had been chumming one area of reef that had a large resident Gray Reef shark population. Gray Reef sharks themselves do not grow to very large proportions. In fact, they are kind of small, reaching only two metres in length.

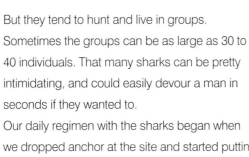

But they tend to hunt and live in groups. Sometimes the groups can be as large as 30 to 40 individuals. That many sharks can be pretty intimidating, and could easily devour a man in seconds if they wanted to.

Our daily regimen with the sharks began when we dropped anchor at the site and started putting on our equipment. Dozens would show up at the boat to investigate. By the time we donned our scuba gear and got into the water, the sharks had left, and we needed to draw them back with chum. Over a couple weeks we had acclimatised the sharks to our presence with frequent visits and tasty snacks to bolster their confidence. In general, however, they acted skittishly around us and we found it frustrating that these animals seemed too frightened by our scuba gear to approach close enough for decent shots.

A group of Lemon sharks crowding the back of the dive boat in the Bahamas where they are being fed fish scraps to bring them close enough for photographs. These shy animals almost never come within camera range without bait.

One morning, I decided to try shooting some video with just my mask, fins and snorkel on as soon as we arrived. I grabbed my stuff as soon as the anchor had been set, and jumped into the water before the sharks left. I started fidgeting with the camera to get everything ready to shoot as the sharks circled me closely. I was so busy with the camera that I didn't realize just how close they were. I also didn't realize the current was silently whisking me away from the boat. When the first shark swam so near that I felt the water move as he passed me, I decided to forget about the camera and take a look around. I had drifted about 30 metres from the boat and the sharks had taken an intense interest in me.

It's interesting to feed sharks down on the reef and watch as they size up the fish you are offering them. Sharks like to be cautious. They often circle a tasty morsel several times before deciding to lunge for it. Then they often lunge, but don't bite. They just bump it a little to see what will happen. If nothing bad happens, then they circle around again and take a bite. A big bite.

My friend Mark Tarczynski makes shark photography look easy in the Bahamas! This Lemon shark is almost performing on command.

Snorkelling on the surface, people look like something dead or dying, something that doesn't belong and might be good to eat. I decided that I would never, ever snorkel with sharks again

A Sand Tiger shark (*Carcharias Taurus*) cruising through the wreck of the Atlas, about 40 km off the coast of North Carolina. These sharks can be found at certain times of the year around a few shipwrecks there. Biologists think they congregate at the wrecks to mate. This is one of the few ways to see sharks without bait.

A Caribbean Reef shark in the Bahamas zooms past me in a blur of motion.

Left: A Tiger shark bites the bait-box, trying to get the fish inside. The plastic milk crates only last a few dives before the sharks tear them apart.

Above: The shark 'feeding frenzy' is a behaviour almost unknown in the wild. When a large amount of food is introduced in the vicinity of a large number of sharks, they may compete violently for food until it is all consumed. However, this rarely happens naturally. Here a large frozen fish was brought down for a group of Caribbean Reef sharks.

It is not so interesting to *be* the tasty morsel. I knew I was in trouble when I realized that the sharks were circling me the way they do when they are about to take a bite. I knew that once they started bumping me, I had very little time before they would start biting. Looking around, I counted dozens of sharks. I started swimming back towards the boat as best I could, while keeping my mask in the water and watching the sharks. I turned around and around to keep an eye on as many as I could. Each time I turned, a shark that had been sneaking up behind me turned and swam off, only to glide back and make a run at me from another direction. The sharks swam all round and under me. I was hopelessly surrounded. I could not take my face out of the water and yell for help because I felt for certain that the short distraction would give a shark an opportunity to get close enough to bite. I quickly glanced up at the boat and yelped through my snorkel. My friends, chatting as they put on their gear, just smiled in my direction, taking my call for help as a gleeful sign that I was getting great shots. One even waved. They had no idea that I was only seconds from being attacked.

When the first shark struck me, I lashed out hard at it. I pushed my camera into its face as hard as I could. The shark took the hit in its stride, turning away and coming back at me from another angle. My memory at this point is fuzzy. I remember screaming loudly through my snorkel, while I bashed, kicked, punched and slammed every shark that came within reach. I used my camera housing as a weapon. At the same time, I swam feebly towards the boat, unable to put much of my effort into swimming. By then, my friends on the boat had realized what was happening. They were trying to start the engines and release the anchor to get to me. I have no idea how long it took, but before they got the boat untied, I made it back. All three of them grabbed me by my wetsuit and pulled me from the water, right up and over the side of the boat. I clearly remember the sharks actually lifting their heads out of the water snapping at me as I was pulled free, almost like a cartoon. I had literally been saved at the last minute from certain death.

Left: **Many people might fear sharks as monsters, but to me they are beautiful, like this Tiger shark.**

Below: **My friend Julia Cichowski swimming with a moderately-sized Tiger shark in the Bahamas.**

These three images show an Oceanic White Tip shark (*Carcharhinus longimanus*) in the waters off Hawaii. These sharks have long pectoral fins to provide extra lift, like aircraft wings, as they swim long distances. Unlike reef sharks, Oceanic White Tips live in the open sea, far from land. The one on the right has a fisherman's hook in its mouth and was lucky to survive. The top left shark has a pilotfish hanging around for free scraps.

I sat on the bottom of the boat and trembled in fear. My adrenaline had been pumping hard to keep me going, but once out of the water, I couldn't stop shaking. My camera's dome port on the lens was ruined, scratched from being repeatedly jammed into the rough skin of the sharks, but I had survived without a scratch. We all laughed nervously, but it wasn't funny. I have two friends, very well-known underwater photographers, who were on separate occasions both severely injured, nearly killed, by a *single* Gray Reef shark that was aggravated. One shark can remove a grapefruit-sized chunk from a person in a single bite. Under such circumstances, a person would bleed to death in minutes. A handful of sharks biting me would have been *very* bad.

The two most infamous sharks on Earth: the Tiger shark (Above) and Great White shark (Right). While the Tiger shark mostly inhabits tropical nearshore waters where it hunts fish and sea turtles, the White shark prefers cooler waters where it hunts seals and sea lions.

Swimming among the sharks with scuba, divers seem to be accepted as something that belongs – loud, and disruptive too, maybe a little scary – but not food. Sharks keep their distance. But on the surface, people look like something dead or dying, something that doesn't belong and might be good to eat. I decided that I would never, ever snorkel with sharks again. This became my number one rule: *don't snorkel with sharks!*

People usually have one of two feelings for sharks. Most people fear them like monsters. A minority of people who watch a lot of Discovery Channel or scuba dive seem to think of them as puppy dogs – not really dangerous. I believe the truth lies between these two extremes. It's *incredibly* unlikely that you will be attacked by a shark, but I still recommend a healthy dose of respect for an animal that *can* eat you if it wants to. They aren't puppy dogs.

Blue sharks (*Prionace glauca*) photographed off the coast of Rhode Island. Blue sharks live in the open ocean and make one of the longest migrations in the animal world. In the Atlantic, they migrate between the coast of the United States in the summer to the coast of Europe in the winter. Tagging studies have proved that the sharks might migrate as much as 8,000 km a year.

I learned a great deal of respect for sharks that day on Kwajalein. I still love sharks, and find them among nature's most fascinating and beautiful animals. The experience never diminished my passion for them, but it did remind me that sharks are predators, and they can be dangerous. Over the years I have been fortunate to dive with many species of sharks all over the world and I have never had another bad experience. To me, they are one of the ultimate big animals in the ocean.

Sharks and their direct predecessors have been swimming in the world's oceans for well over 350 million years. Primordial sharks hunted the seas many millions of years before dinosaurs walked the Earth. Following a period of intense evolutionary experimentation, the basic shark we know today emerged about 250 million years ago. While they continue to evolve like all animals, the fact that sharks have survived for so long with the same basic design demonstrates the incredible effectiveness of their anatomy.

Left: This Blue shark (*Prionace glauca*) has been permanently disfigured by a fisherman. When sharks are caught on a hook, sometimes fishermen slash the mouth of the shark to get rid of it. Often the shark dies, but sometimes the shark can survive with its wounds. It's better than becoming shark fin soup.

Reaching up to 15 m in length and 12,000 kg, the Whale shark (*Rhincodon typus*) is the largest fish in the world, yet it is completely harmless to people. It feeds on plankton and schools of small fish. Although the shark's mouth may exceed two metres across, its throat is comparatively small and it couldn't swallow a human even if it wanted to.

Sharks are fish, contained within the taxonomic class called *Chondrichthyes* (meaning cartilage-fish). This class of fish contains over 800 species worldwide, including over 400 species of sharks and 350 species of rays and skates, which are basically just flattened sharks. Sharks and rays come in many shapes and sizes. The largest fish in the ocean is, in fact, the tremendous Whale shark, reaching about

15 metres in length. The smallest known shark grows to only 25 centimetres long at full size.

Sharks and their close relatives (rays, skates, and ratfish) differ from the bony fish in many ways. Among the more obvious, sharks and their relatives have cartilaginous skeletons, and lack swim bladders. The cartilaginous skeleton makes the shark more flexible than similarly-sized bony fish.

The largest fish in the ocean is, in fact, the tremendous Whale shark, reaching about 15 metres in length

At up to 12 metres long, the Basking shark (*Cetorhinus maximus*) is the second largest fish on Earth (right behind the Whale shark). It can reach 4,500 kg but survives on nothing but tiny planktonic crustaceans called copepods which it filters from the water with comb-like sieves on its gills.

The shark's lack of a swim bladder means that, unlike bony fish, the shark tends to sink. A bony fish uses an organ called a swim bladder to maintain neutral buoyancy, so it can hover like a hot air balloon. The fish adds or removes gas from the bladder through its bloodstream to change its buoyancy. A shark has a large, oil-rich liver that provides some buoyancy, but not enough to keep it from sinking. The Basking shark's liver can weigh as much as 25 per cent of the total weight of its body. To stay off the bottom, sharks have to keep moving. While the shark uses its tail fin in a back and forth motion to provide forward thrust, its pectoral fins work like aircraft wings to provide lift. As long as the fins move forward through the water, they keep the shark up. This lack of a swim bladder is not necessarily a weakness. Bony fish cannot ascend too quickly because the expanding gas in the swim bladder would cause it to rupture. They can only ascend as fast as they can remove the gas from it. By not having one, sharks can swim straight up as fast as they like without any danger of hurting themselves.

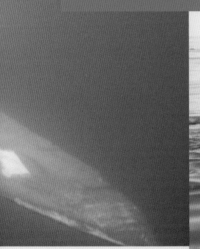

Right: Like a massive swimming pool skimmer, a Whale shark in Mexico scoops plankton from just under the surface of the water.

Below: A pile of White-tip Reef sharks (*Triaenodon obesus*) resting under a coral overhang in the Galapagos Islands. These sharks hunt at night and rest during the day.

Not too long ago, scientists thought all sharks had to swim at all times, not just to stay off the bottom, but to keep water moving over their gills. It turns out that many species of sharks sometimes stop swimming and rest on the bottom, gulping water to ventilate their gills.

Bottom-dwelling species of sharks like the Nurse shark (*Ginglymostoma cirratus*) actually live their entire lives on or near the bottom. Sharks are a diverse group of fish with many specializations for survival. They inhabit all of the world's oceans, from the arctic to the

Right: Another nocturnal shark, the Nurse shark (*Ginglymostoma cirratum*), resting on the bottom in the Caribbean.

tropics, from the surface to the deep-sea, and from the shoreline to the open ocean. Some species, like the Bull shark (*Carcharhinus leucas*) can even swim up into freshwater rivers and lakes, hundreds of miles from the ocean.

Above: People used to think that sharks had to keep swimming or they would suffocate. Now we know that many species of sharks can rest and gulp water to ventilate their gills like this White-tip Reef shark.

Bottom-dwelling species, like the Nurse shark, actually live their entire lives on or near the sea bottom

The Caribbean Reef shark (*Carcharhinus perezi*) doesn't look very toothy at first glance. Its teeth are hidden when its mouth is closed. But this shark has an impressive set of teeth that can take huge bites out of its prey. This robust shark reaches three metres.

This female Great white shark is covered in cuts and scars all over her head and gills from mating. In sharks this is a violent affair where the male holds the female by her pectoral fins using his teeth. Her skin is twice as thick as a male's skin to protect her.

Since sharks are an ancient group of animals, people often assume that they are primitive in some way, but this assumption couldn't be further from the truth. With such a long evolutionary history, sharks have had plenty of time to refine themselves. Recent studies have shown sharks to be remarkably sophisticated. For example, most sharks have an incredible sense of smell. Extrapolations of experiments on shark smell have suggested that some can detect one drop of blood dissolved in as much as four million litres of water. Such a keenly developed sense of smell leaves no doubt that a shark has few rivals in the nose department.

Sharks also have senses we can't even begin to experience. They have an electrosensory system that allows them to detect the extremely minute bio-electrical currents generated, for example, by the muscles of a swimming fish. The snout of a shark is covered in tiny pores called *Ampullae of Lorenzini*, filled with a jelly-like substance leading to nerve cells. The Ampullae of Lorenzini convert electrical impulses in the water to an electrical signal in the shark's nerves. Therefore the shark can 'feel' extremely tiny electrical currents in the water. To put the sensitivity of this electrosensory system in perspective, imagine connecting wires to a nine volt transistor radio battery and separating the ends of the wires by a kilometre. Some sharks can detect that electrical current. At close range, a fish hiding in a hole is betrayed by the electrical signature of its own heart beating.

In the 1980's heavy fishing for Sand Tiger sharks (*Carcharias Taurus*) dramatically reduced the number of these sharks in the Atlantic ocean. Virtually none were seen in North Carolina for many years. Today, Sand Tigers are protected by law in the U.S., Australia and other countries, and they are making a comeback.

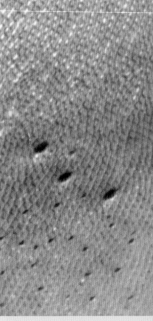

Some sharks can 'hear' the tiny pressure variations generated by an injured fish struggling to swim. They don't do this with the kind of hearing we humans have (eardrums), but with a system common to many fish called a *lateral line*. Along the sides of a shark, a series of pores contains small capsules, each containing a tiny hair-like fibre. Very small changes in water pressure cause the fibres to move, sending a signal to the shark. It learns to recognize the feel of different kinds of pressure variations, such as those caused by a struggling injured fish off in the distance, too far away to see. The shark then knows possible food is nearby and begins to search for the fish. Many people mistakenly believe that sharks have poor eyesight. Most in fact have excellent eyesight, and many have simply incredible low-light vision. A shiny mirror-like layer located behind the retina called the *tapetum lucidum* reflects light back through the retina a second time, increasing its sensitivity. At night, the eyes of these sharks reflect light the same way the eyes of cats do because cats and sharks share similar low-light adaptations of eyesight. Many sharks like to hunt at dawn and dusk, because they can see their prey much better than the prey can see them.

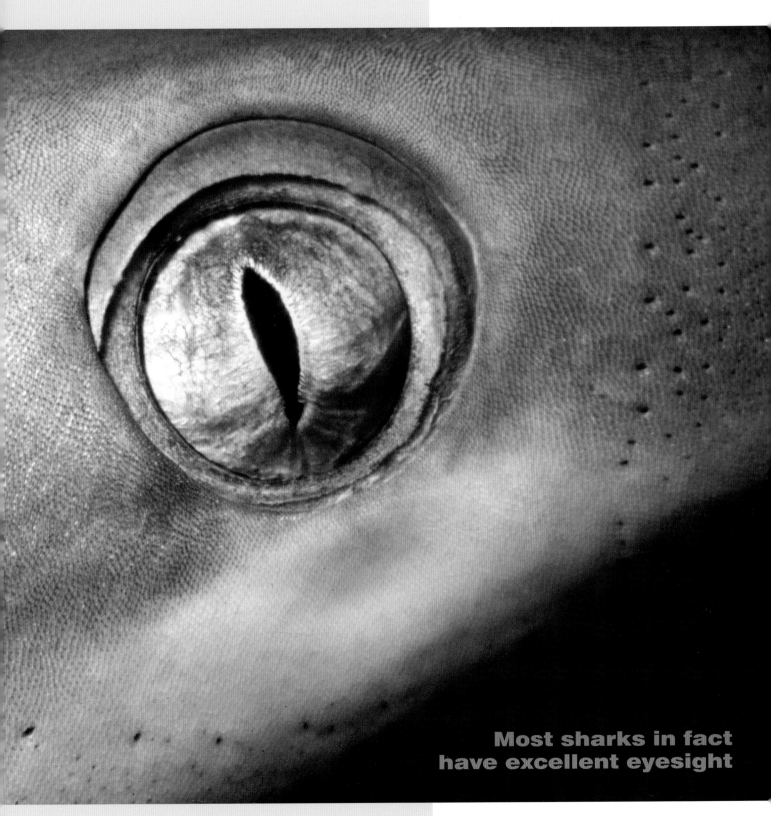

Most sharks in fact have excellent eyesight

Right: The sharp, triangular teeth of a Gray Reef shark are designed for cutting so the shark can take big bites out of larger prey.

Below: Like a Basking shark, a Manta Ray (*Manta birostris*) feeds on plankton by filtering it from the water with gills that act like strainers.

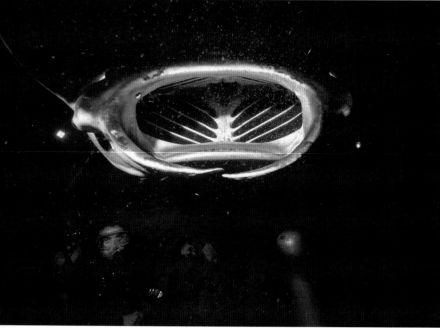

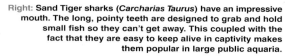

Right: Sand Tiger sharks (*Carcharias Taurus*) have an impressive mouth. The long, pointy teeth are designed to grab and hold small fish so they can't get away. This coupled with the fact that they are easy to keep alive in captivity makes them popular in large public aquaria.

Far Right: Some sharks, such as this Silky shark (*Carcharhinus falciformis*), can be put into a kind of hypnotic state called *tonic immobility* by turning them upside down and holding their tail just right. Nobody is quite sure why this happens.

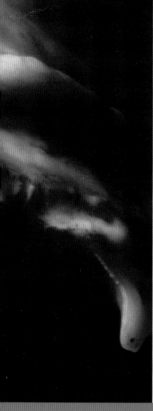

Sharks never need to go to a dentist, since they don't really care about cavities. They have many rows of teeth. The first row of teeth is used until they get dull or break. Then they fall out and new ones rotate into place from the next row back as if the teeth were on a conveyor belt. For the entire life of a shark, it never runs out of new teeth, and never worries about the teeth it has. In addition to teeth in its mouth, a shark also has a kind of teeth on its skin, called *dermal denticles*. These, like the scales on a bony fish, all point towards the tail. Water flows smoothly over them as the shark swims. A hand brushed from head to tail over the skin of the shark will detect a reasonably smooth surface. But brush a hand backwards from tail to head and the skin feels very rough, like sandpaper. The dermal denticles make the skin of a shark incredibly tough.

Sharks smell better than us, hear better than us, see better than us in low light, recognize electrical signals to which we are completely blind and have perfect teeth. These are certainly not the attributes of a primitive animal. It's no coincidence that they are top predators in the ocean.

Unfortunately, sharks only have a small number of offspring at a time, and they take a long time to reach sexual maturity. As a result, their populations do not recover quickly from overfishing. Today, sharks face incredible pressure from the shark-finning industry. Sharks are caught just for their fins, which are worth a lot of money as the prime ingredient in shark fin soup, popular in China and other far eastern countries. Often sharks are thrown back alive, with their fins removed, so that they die a slow and painful death. It's not only wasteful, but cruel. Today, the shark-finning industry is killing sharks at an unprecedented rate to feed the demand for shark fin soup in a blossoming Chinese economy. The situation is far more dire than most people realize – sharks are critically endangered. Unfortunately, sharks are not cute and fuzzy like pandas, so it's hard to get people interested in the need to protect them. But we must.

Below: The remote and rough waters around Darwin Island in the Galapagos are home to massive schools of Scalloped Hammerhead sharks (*Sphyrna lewini*). These large schools become harder and harder to see every year. Shark finning is taking its toll on these beautiful animals.

Scalloped Hammerheads (*Sphyrna lewini*) often school around the shallows in order to be cleaned by smaller fish. Here a crew of King Angelfish (*Holacanthus passer*) clean a hammerhead that is hovering in the current. Cleaning helps the sharks get rid of parasites and provides a meal for the cleaner fishes.

Unfortunately, sharks are not cute and fuzzy like pandas, so it's hard to get people interested in the need to protect them. But we must

An ocean without sharks is an ocean missing a critical component of the food chain. As predators at the very top of the chain, sharks fill an important niche. Because most sharks lack the speed or manoeuvrability of their prey, they go after the sick, weak or unwary. This way, sharks help keep the gene pool of their prey healthy. Search as you may, you won't find a school of near-sighted mackerel since they would be devoured quickly by sharks and other predators. Such an undesirable gene cannot exist in the presence of such tough competition. Predators like sharks constantly improve the health of ocean ecosystems by eating whatever they can catch (and not eating what they can't catch). The slow, sick or near-sighted fish become dinner for a shark and never pass on undesirable genes. This is by no means unique in the animal world – terrestrial predators perform the same role. A lack of sharks in any ocean ecosystem could be disastrous to the health of ocean food chains, including the ones we rely upon for food resources.

Rays are basically just flattened sharks with wings. Their gills are under their body. Manta rays (bottom) used to be called the Devil rays because of the cephalic fins that look like horns. Sailors thought they were dangerous sea monsters. In reality, the ray uses the cephalic fins to help scoop up plankton.

Above: Eagle rays feed mostly on clams, snails and other molluscs they dig up in the bottom.

Right: At a popular dive site called *Stingray City* in Grand Cayman, people can feed the stingrays which have been acclimatised to people. Here my buddy David Keefe feeds a piece of squid to a stingray.

If protecting sharks for environmental purposes isn't convincing enough, perhaps we should protect sharks for more selfish reasons – what we can learn from them to help ourselves. Research on sharks may someday provide medicines and cures for a variety of diseases. Their highly-evolved immune system is strongly resistant to many illnesses including cancer. Perhaps the best argument in favour of protecting sharks is simply that they are wild animals and have just as much of a right to survive as we do. They have been living on this planet hundreds of millions of years longer than we have. What right do we have to hunt them to extinction? What effects would it have on the environment if we did? The ocean's ecosystems cannot survive without sharks. We must respect these animals and give them the space they need to live. After all, we actually need them a lot more than they need us.

Above: **The Tasseled Wobbegong shark (*Eucrossorhinus dasypogon*) looks very different from what most people imagine as a shark. It lives camouflaged on the bottom, blending silently into the sea floor and patiently waiting for unwary fish to swim by. Then, it lunges and gulps down its unsuspecting prey.**

Below: **This Southern Stingray (*Dasyatis Americana*), a bottom-dwelling ray, is feeding in the sand. Like a swimming metal detector, it finds worms and clams in the sand using its keen electrosensory system, then slurps them up. It's mouth is underneath its body.**

WHALES AND DOLPHINS

My friend Glen Holmes is dwarfed by an adult
female Sperm whale (*Physeter macrocephalus*)
in the Caribbean waters of Dominica.

Inset: Dolphins travel in groups called pods.
A pod of curious Atlantic Spotted dolphins
(*Stenella frontalis*) in the waters of the Bahamas.

Many years ago, I escaped the harsh New England winter on a week-long holiday in the Turks & Caicos Islands to enjoy some warm water diving with the possibility of some nice pictures of reefs and sea creatures. I spent most of the week shooting with my macro lens, which is designed for making images of small stuff at high magnification. One morning on the way to the dive site, a strange shadow under the boat caught my eye. The captain saw it too, and did a double take. We soon realized that a humpback whale was directly below us. Upon further inspection, we could see she had a calf. By the time the captain had suggested I might want to try slipping quietly into the water with my snorkel gear, I had already suited up. Unfortunately for me, my camera was fitted with a lens that could only photograph something under a couple of centimetres long and I had no other lenses with me on the boat. I left the camera aboard and gently slipped into the water. It was the first time I had ever found myself face to face with a whale. In the distance I could hear the groans and moans of a male Humpback 'singing'. Directly in front of me in the deep blue of the Caribbean, a mother Humpback whale sized me up and put a protective flipper over her calf. It is one of the most tender things I have ever seen. She soon wandered off, not in a rush, but certainly aware that several other people had jumped into the water and invaded her space. I have been kicking myself ever since for not having a wide angle lens with me on the boat and I try not to let that happen again.

Far left: I free-dived down about 24 metres to photograph this sleeping Humpback whale (*Megaptera novaeangliae*) in the Silver Banks, Dominican Republic.

Left and below: An inquisitive Humpback whale approaches the boat in the ocean off Massachusetts, USA. Humpbacks are one of the most curious of the large whales. In areas where whale-watching boats regularly operate, such as Hawaii and Massachusetts, the whales have become used to visitors. The white bumps on the whale's head are barnacles.

The similarities between humans and whales are striking and we are both the most intelligent animals in our respective worlds

Atlantic Spotted dolphins have become accustomed to swimmers and snorkelers in the waters of Little Bahama Bank and they frequently play with people for hours on end. But keeping up with playful dolphins can be exhausting, as my friend Audrey Brown is discovering!

At first glance, a whale may not seem to bear much resemblance to us, but the similarities between humans and whales are striking. On the taxonomic scale, both of us are mammals, a class of vertebrates sharing many characteristics. For example, we are both warm blooded, bear live young and feed them milk. Even more obviously, we both have lungs and breathe air. Yet we share other traits that go beyond simple taxonomy. We both care for and protect our offspring for a fairly long time. We both have a social system involving friends and families. And we are both the most intelligent animals in our respective worlds.

Unfortunately, our knowledge of whales and dolphins is limited. From the fossil record, we know that all members of the order *Cetacea* (whales and dolphins) evolved from four-legged land mammals about a hundred million years ago, long before humans walked the earth. From those early beginnings, the early cetaceans adapted to their aquatic environment through millions of years of evolution. They slowly lost their hind limbs, while the tail evolved into a fluke. The fingers or toes on their front limbs became webbed, eventually metamorphosing into the flippers we see today. To the present day skeletons of whales and dolphins still have finger bones left over from those ancient lost fingers.

My wife Christine shot this stunning photograph of a Humpback whale and her calf at the Silver Banks in the Dominican Republic. The calf doesn't seem small at 5 metres in length, but the mother is over 12 metres long. Calves are nursed by their mothers for at least a year.

As time went on, the whales branched out into two different groups, each specializing in feeding on different prey. One group kept its teeth, becoming what we call the *Odontoceti* ('toothed') whales. Today, the sub-order Odontoceti includes such animals as the Sperm whale, the Orca and the Bottlenose dolphin. Some people find it surprising to learn that dolphins are just small, toothed whales. These toothed whales actively hunt and feed on prey using their sharp teeth. But another group of ancestral whales found a different niche in the food chain. Exploiting the incredible amount of zooplankton in certain areas of the oceans, the whales of the suborder *Mysticetes* lost their teeth and developed baleen. These are large plates growing in rows from the top of a whale's mouth like so many combs. They are made of keratin, the same substance of which the human fingernail is made. This stiff but flexible comb-like arrangement functions as a filter or strainer, allowing water to pass through, but capturing animals like small fish, krill, or copepods. Filter feeding allows baleen whales to eat tons of food every day, all without teeth. In this ironic twist of evolution, the largest creatures on Earth feed on some of the smallest.

Left: A pair of Atlantic Spotted dolphins is hunting in the sand for razor fish and flounder. They use clicks from their echolocation to 'see' objects hiding in the sand.

Above: A Beluga whale (*Delphinapterus leucas*) stares back and me and vocalizes in the green waters of the St. Lawrence river, Canada. Often called sea canaries for their bird-like voices, Belugas are very talkative – if only we knew what they were saying.

The transformation from land animal to marine animal is perhaps nowhere more pronounced than in the body form of the cetaceans. All have assumed a hydrodynamic shape to allow them to pass through the water with as little resistance as possible. Dolphins have long been the envy of scientists attempting to produce fast submarines with low drag. Some dolphins can swim at speeds of 50 kilometres per hour.

Using echolocation, their clicks bounce back to the animal giving it a mental picture of the object, from its distance, size, and location to its density and thickness

Male dolphins often hang out in groups away from the females. Like a group of teenagers having fun, these three adolescent Atlantic Spotted dolphins taunted me and investigated my camera for several minutes in the Bahamas.

Below: Dolphins are always smiling. They can't help it – it's the shape of their face. But don't let the smile fool you. The mouth of this Bottlenose dolphin (*Tursiops truncatus*) is full of sharp teeth and if it is aggravated, it will bite.

In a world where light doesn't travel very far, eyesight is of very limited use to whales and dolphins. This is not to say that they cannot see well, because they can. But their 'visual' world is a world of sound. Sound travels four times faster in water than it does in air, and it travels further too. Many whales and dolphins navigate and hunt using a system called echolocation. The animal produces a series of clicks which travels through the water and bounces off distant underwater objects. The clicks echoing back at the animal give it a mental picture of the object, from its distance, size, and location to its density and thickness. Using this natural form of sonar, the dolphin, for example, can even see fish hiding under a layer of sand on the sea bottom.

The False Killer whale (*Pseudorca crassidens*) is a large dolphin that reaches 6 metres long and is often known to be rather aggressive. It even feeds on other dolphins at times, though it seems to prefer fish. These tropical animals can be curious, sometimes approaching boats, and occasionally, divers. I never felt threatened by these animals as they buzzed me a few times for a look.

Many whales and dolphins seem to use sound in their social lives as a form of communication. For example, Humpback whales sing songs (whose meaning we do not understand) while many dolphins make squeaks and chirps. Blue whales make loud underwater sounds which travel great distances, and may enable them to hear each other over thousands of kilometres. Every year, millions of people get a close look at whales by going on whale-watching trips. This form of tourism has given people a new-found appreciation for these gentle giants of the seas. We can only hope that as we continue to better understand and appreciate whales and dolphins, we will come to realize that they should be cherished and fully protected the world over. Who knows, perhaps some day we will learn something important *from* them, not just about them.

Spotted dolphins often play follow the leader, where one animal leads the way and others follow behind in chase. In the warm waters of the Bahamas, this group races towards the sunlit surface for a breath of air.

Below: In the calm waters in the lee of the tall island of Dominica, Sperm whales find both deep water for hunting and calm surface conditions for raising their young. A year-round population of these whales thrives just offshore, where mothers give birth to their calves.

Right: This Sperm whale might look as if it is about to eat my buddy Glen, but these whales fortunately prefer to hunt giant squid down in the abyss.

In Herman Melville's classic novel, a Sperm whale called Moby Dick sinks ships and kills sailors. This is the reputation Sperm whales have acquired over the years, perhaps because of their large size and huge teeth. Whalers always saw the violent side of whales, understandably since they were basically fighting for their lives whenever whalers were around.

When not faced with the business end of a harpoon, Sperm whales are not dangerous to people. They are the largest toothed animals on the planet, and perhaps the most abundant of the great whales, but we rarely get to study them because they spend so much time underwater. Sperm whales dive deep, holding their breath as they descend to feed on deep-sea squid and fish. They spend 90 per cent of their lives down in the abyss where they can't be seen. Only rarely do these energetic animals take a break and rest at the surface. A few years back, I ventured to the tiny island

Above and right: Although most whales and dolphins are grey or black in colour, the Beluga is white, helping it to blend in to its arctic sea-ice habitat. Most Belugas are wary of people and very hard to photograph underwater. This curious female found me interesting and swam up to investigate.

Far right: Reaching a massive 18 metres, the Northern Right whale (*Eubalaena glacialis*) is the most endangered whale in the world. There are just 300 of them left. This one was photographed at the summer feeding grounds in the Bay of Fundy, Canada.

nation of Dominica in the Caribbean to attempt to meet and photograph these giants. In the winter, large male Sperm whales migrate to the island to meet up with the groups of females which tend to stay near there all year around. They get together to mate, but also seem to spend more time than usual playing and relaxing. I hoped I could get close enough for some underwater encounters.

My plane landed in Dominica and I was immediately seized by the beauty of the island – lush tropical rainforests, soaring mountains, deep valleys plummeting to the sea and waterfalls everywhere. As we flew in low over the treetops, I could see the banana trees lined up in neat rows along the narrow roads. If Eden exists, it surely must be Dominica – an undiscovered paradise such as you could only imagine. After the usual luggage hassles and getting to my hotel, I prepared for the expedition, readying all my cameras and checking everything twice.

I was lucky to be working with a private charter boat captained by an island local who knew where to find the whales. The next morning we left the dock with the sun getting higher in the sky. Whales might be big, but they aren't easy to find. Sperm whales are even harder to find than other species because they don't stick out of the water very much and their distinctive blow is small and easily missed. Unlike most whales, whose spouts shoot straight up high into the air, the spout of the Sperm whale points to the left and forward. It doesn't spray up more than two or three metres, making it hard to spot from a distance.

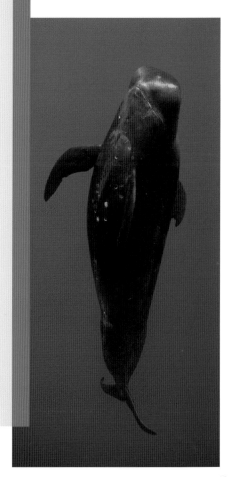

Left: This male Bottlenose dolphin exhibits scratches on its body from the teeth of other dolphins. Male dolphins often fight by raking their teeth against each other, leaving scars.

Below: Off Hawaii, a Short-finned Pilot whale (*Globicephala macrorhynchus*) is hanging vertically in the water column, staring at me. The massive rounded forehead, called a melon, is used to focus the intense sound waves this whale uses for echolocation.

Knowing this made it even more incredible when captain Dave yelled down from the top of the boat that he could see some whales – and we had only searched for an hour. I scanned the horizon in the direction he pointed, but saw nothing. I thought he was kidding me, but sure enough, ten minutes later as the boat drew closer to the whales, I could see them.

A pod of Atlantic Spotted dolphins doing what they like to do best: goof off. These social and gregarious animals spend a large percentage of their time just having fun.

Inset: Two Atlantic Spotted dolphins doing something else that dolphins love to do: mating. Dolphins are one of the only animals besides humans that engage in intercourse just for the fun of it.

The whales appeared very still, just relaxing on the surface. A large female and her calf, half her length, floated quietly as we approached. This behaviour is appropriately called 'logging', because a resting Sperm whale looks just like a floating log at the surface. Yet, as we got within range where I might be able to get into the water and swim to them, the female raised her mammoth head out of the water (a common behaviour in some whales, called a spy hop), gave us a look, and started swimming the other way. We did not pursue them because it was obvious they weren't interested in our company. I started to understand how difficult this might be!

Some people find it surprising to learn that dolphins are just small, toothed whales

Within minutes, Dave had found another group, again a mother and calf. We were actually in front of the whales when we spotted them, so we just cut the boat's engine to see what they would do. Drifting quietly in the light breeze, we could hear the blows of the whales as they continued to approach. I grabbed my camera and slid quietly over the side, making my way towards the whales using only mask, fins and snorkel. I couldn't see them, but the clicks of their echolocation gave them away.

Down in the depths, where there is no light, Sperm whales hunt using echolocation. The only problem with echolocation is that it can also give away the presence of the whale if the prey hears it. Lucky for Sperm whales that their favourite food – giant squid – can't hear. As I swam through the water, my eyes played tricks. The bright noon sun penetrated the cobalt blue sea in dancing bright shafts. As a whale begins to appear out of the blue, it first resembles just a shadow. Slowly it comes into view, taking shape as if materializing out of nowhere. As the pair of shapes approached, I could make out the jaw line and blunt heads.

The first sight I see when I jump off the back of the dive boat into water filled with wild dolphins – they all come over to check out the goofy human who can barely swim compared to them.

An Atlantic Spotted dolphin
with its rostrum plunged into
the sand to grab a tasty morsel.

Success! The
dolphin grabbed
a small flounder
in the sand.

Soon I could see the wrinkled-looking skin behind the head. When the calf saw me, there was a definite reaction. It pulled out of formation from behind its mother and came a little closer to me. But mom was having none of this. She kept her eye on me and picked up the pace. The calf had no choice but to continue. I shot about half a roll of film of them as they passed, but I was too far away for any good shots. I knew that to really see these whales, they were going to have to come to *me*.

The next morning we tried again. This time we found a pod of five whales. Two mothers, two calves and a big male swam slowly at the surface. They didn't appear in a hurry to get anywhere, just lolling along taking their time. As we approached, they made no effort to swim away from us. We eased the boat a few hundred metres ahead of them and I slipped into the water. The whales came right up and swam past me as if I weren't there. I clicked the shutter as fast as I could. The big male stayed about 10 metres below me. I held my breath and tried to dive down to him, but he simply moved a little deeper, keeping himself just out of reach. I was amazed by how effortlessly he seemed to control his buoyancy, simply rising and sinking with no apparent effort, to remain exactly the same distance from me.

Left: An Atlantic Spotted dolphin leaps from the water on its way to the bow of the boat for a free ride.

In the foreground, a mature Atlantic Spotted dolphin, showing its namesake spots. But these dolphins don't start to get them until they are about four years old. The younger dolphin behind has no spots yet.

The Sperm whale gets its name from the spermaceti organ which fills most of its huge head. In the 18th and 19th centuries, New England whalers sought out the Sperm whale for its valuable spermaceti oil, which makes an exceptionally fine lubricant. Nobody is absolutely sure what the spermaceti organ actually does for the whale, but there are two prevalent theories. One suggests that the organ is used to focus and control the beam of sound that the whale uses for echolocation. The other theory proposes that the organ serves as a buoyancy control device. The waxy oil within the organ has a melting point of about 45 degrees Celsius. By controlling blood flow to the organ (and therefore its temperature), the whale may be able to adjust the density (and therefore buoyancy) of the spermaceti. If the wax is cooler, it contracts and becomes denser, making the whale sink better. When warmed, the wax expands, making the whale less dense. This technique could be a way of assisting the whale with diving and ascending. For all we know, both theories could be right.

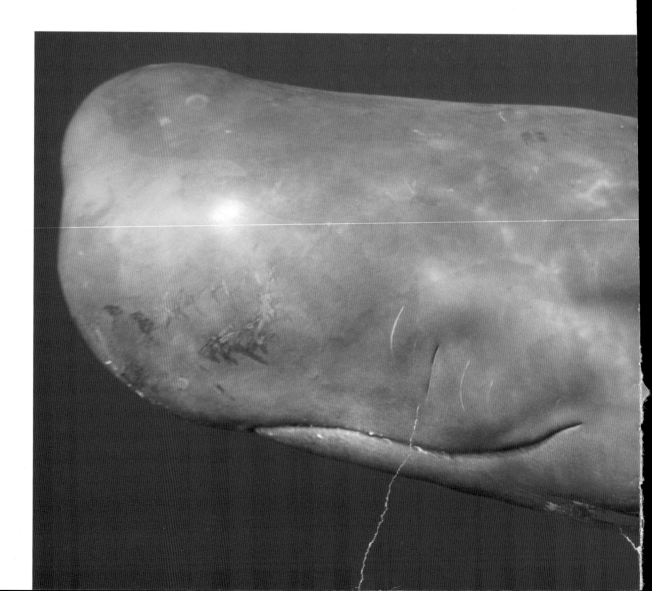

The Sperm whale gets its name from the spermaceti organ which fills most of its huge head – nobody is absolutely sure what this organ actually does for the whale

As the whales slowly swam out of view, I hopped back into the boat and we slowly caught up with them again. With the engine shut off, I got up on the top deck and took a few surface shots. The whales kept coming closer and closer to the boat until they were too close for my telephoto lens. They drifted to within a few metres of the boat. Dave called my attention to the situation: "Hey Jonathan, you better get in the water *now*!"
I grabbed my camera and lowered myself into

Although dolphins can see and hear very well, they cannot smell. They lack both olfactory nerves and an olfactory lobe in the brain. So in spite of its name, the Bottlenose dolphin doesn't actually have a nose at all.

the water right next to a whale. Male Sperm whales can reach more than 18 metres long, while the females are considerably smaller, reaching about 12 metres. But even the six metre-long calves look big to me. The whale and I looked right at each other, separated by only about three metres. He rolled to keep me in view. The Sperm whale has a relatively small eye as whales go, and it cannot rotate much in its socket, so the whale must turn its entire body to look in different directions.

The Bottlenose dolphin has been demonstrated to be extremely intelligent – perhaps more so than monkeys and apes. This pair is checking out the camera.

This series of images shows the 'Bandana Game' in full swing. Captain Scott offers up a bandana to the dolphins. They take it and play keep-away from each other and the divers. The animals can carry it on their fluke, rostrum or pectoral fins. Who needs hands?

As I continued to float there in awe of the massive size of the male, the other whales came closer for a look at me. After my experiences with whales swimming away from me the day before, this seemed like a stroke of incredible luck. I fired frame after frame. Eventually the whales swam away. I swam back to the boat, wondering what, if anything, the whales thought about me. At between 12 and 18 kilogrammes, the brain of a Sperm whale is the largest on the planet. Who knows what they do with such a big brain? Are they smart? If so, how could we tell? Biologists have suggested that the massive brain may be designed for the complicated echolocation system, but they clearly are curious, as was demonstrated only moments later.

A mother
Atlantic Spotted
dolphin and
her calf.

A pregnant
Atlantic Spotted
dolphin, showing
her bulging belly.

A pair of Bottlenose dolphins in the Caribbean. This is one of the most adaptable species of dolphins, living anywhere from near shore to far out at sea and from the tropics to temperate waters. If this dolphin looks familiar it might be because 'Flipper' of television fame was a Bottlenose dolphin.

I climbed back into the boat. Yet, before I had even changed film, the whales returned. With only 12 frames left, I got back in the water. I used the rest of the film quickly and called back to the boat for another camera. My wife Christine jumped in the water with my other camera and brought it to me. We swapped cameras just as one of the calves came up to within a metre of me and began clicking its echolocation right at my chest. The clicks are so loud that you can actually feel them in your body. CLICK, CLICK, CLICK went the whale. CLICK went the camera. I wonder if the whale understood me?

At one point, the male rolled over and opened its mouth, revealing its strange arrangement of teeth. The Sperm whale has a mouth full of conical teeth located only in the lower jaw. They fit into sockets in the roof of the mouth. They look pretty mean, but probably aren't all that important in feeding. Most of the items recovered from Sperm whale stomachs are not even chewed, but swallowed whole. An intact 12 metre-long giant squid weighing 200 kilogrammes was recovered from a Sperm whale. Sperm whales with severely mangled jaws have been seen in perfect health, apparently catching food just fine without

Anyone who sees a whale up close will understand why I am so fond of them, and why they should be protected

the complete use of their teeth. This doesn't mean that the giant squid doesn't fight back. Many Sperm whales carry life-long scars from encounters with squid, including big sucker marks on their heads and snouts caused by the squid's sucker disks, which contain sharp hooks to dig into their prey.

Strangely, I never felt at all threatened by the whales. Their patient curiosity seemed completely non-aggressive. The calf which clicked me must have been 'seeing' my body structure well. The clicks bounce off things like lungs and bones with densities different to the surrounding water. Did the calf realize that I was an air-breathing mammal like itself? Who knows what was going through its head. I held my breath and dived down. The calf watched and finally followed, sinking slowly. Soon, I ran out of breath and shot to the surface to breathe, but the calf just floated below me, apparently totally relaxed.

Because of an uncanny ability to store oxygen in their blood and muscles efficiently, adult Sperm whales can stay submerged for well over an hour without taking a breath. They have been tracked by sonar diving to depths of 1,200 metres. However, one Sperm whale caught by a whaling ship in water 3,000 metres deep had a bottom-dwelling shark in its stomach, leading researchers to believe that the Sperm whale can dive a lot deeper than seems possible. Just as amazing is how fast the whales can reach that depth. In one study, a Sperm whale descended at an astonishing 170 metres per minute.

Left and below:
These Atlantic Spotted dolphins are around four years old, the age at which spots start to appear.

Below right:
A pair of Atlantic Spotted dolphins engaged in courtship behaviour. Dolphins are very tactile and like to touch each other a lot.

An adolescent Atlantic Spotted dolphin swimming
around me to show off and engage me in play.

Right: Atlantic Spotted dolphins can zip around underwater
faster than most boats can cruise on the surface. These
animals have been clocked at 40 km per hour.

It's hard to imagine swimming face to face with a creature the size of a bus and an eye larger than a tea cup. But looking a Sperm whale in the eye and watching it look back would convince anyone that we should not be hunting these incredible animals. The Sperm whale probably has one of the most stable populations of any whale on Earth, possibly more than a million. This means that the Sperm whale is the *only* great whale species that is not endangered.

During the 1970's, the Save the Whale campaign brought the plight of whales to international attention. Many people now believe that whales have been saved. But this couldn't be further from the truth. All around the world, whaling still exists. Many countries continue to hunt whales, in spite of international treaties to protect them.

In New England, Hawaii, Alaska and many other places where whales are common, the whale-watching industry has been proved to make far better financial sense than whale hunting. Once a whale is killed, it is gone. But watching whales preserves not only the whales themselves, but the industry and the income.

A huge pod of Bottlenose dolphins swims along with the boat in the open sea off the Galapagos Islands. Their jumping and splashing certainly seemed as if it were designed to impress us.

I would encourage anyone even remotely interested in whales to go on a whale watch and see a whale up close. There is nothing like the experience of seeing a whale of any species in the flesh. Anyone who sees one of these creatures close up will understand why I am so fond of them, and why they should be protected.

A Sperm whale resting at the surface between hour-long deep dives for food.

WEST INDIAN MANATEES

WEST INDIAN MANATEES

Above: West Indian manatees (*Trichechus manatus*) move so slowly that they often have a layer of algae growing on their skin, like this animal in Crystal River, Florida.

Right: Manatees are marine mammals, and like all mammals they have lungs and breathe air. They sip air from the surface through nostrils on their snouts, which can close underwater.

In 1493, Columbus entered into his logbook the sighting of a mermaid in the Caribbean. He wrote that the mermaid was not as beautiful as sailors had been led to believe. Of course, he had not actually seen a mermaid, but instead a manatee, and his logbook became the first written historical reference to the now greatly endangered West Indian manatee (*Trichechus manatus*). The manatee is a marine mammal, like a seal or a whale, but is unique in many ways. Like all mammals, they have lungs and breathe air. Therefore manatees must hold their breath while diving, and need to surface for air periodically. They have a horizontally flattened tail fluke and a pair of front flippers like whales have. But unlike whales, manatees can live in both salt water and fresh water, and move between the two at will.

Manatees are contained within the taxonomic order Sirenia. The term is a reference to the mythical siren of Homer's *Odyssey* – a beautiful mermaid who lured sailors to treacherous waters and reefs. There are only four living species of manatees in the world, all of which are similar in size and appearance, but with minor differences in anatomy.

The West Indian manatee lives throughout the Caribbean and Florida. During the summer, this curious animal roams the coastal ocean as far north as the Carolinas or as far south as Brazil, and throughout the Gulf of Mexico. During winter, however, low water temperature causes the manatees to seek warmer regions. Manatees cannot tolerate water much below 20 degrees Celsius. In winter, when the ocean water temperature drops below that, many manatees go inland, travelling up rivers and canals, to gather near sources of warm water. Natural warm-water springs occur throughout Florida in places where pure, clear water, heated deep within the Earth's crust, flows to the surface. This is generally the only place where large congregations of manatees can be found, since during the warmer months they do not normally gather or travel in groups as do dolphins or whales. The manatees wait out the cold weather in the warm water, and return to the coastal ocean in the spring. I have been to Florida to photograph the manatees half a dozen times. I keep going back because I really love these gentle animals. Every time I swim with them, I remember my first time. It was a cool winter morning. Winter in Florida is not very cold by most standards, but it can get chilly at night. At the crack of dawn I got up and headed out into the chilly morning air, before the sun was even over the horizon. I donned my wetsuit, and gently lowered myself off my rented boat into the dark, murky water of a Florida canal. The water felt cold when it hit my skin, but a few minutes later I was fine. I realized that

the water, at 22 degrees Celsius, was quite a bit warmer than the air.

I gathered up the camera, put my face into the water and looked down. I could see nothing. My kicking had swirled up all kinds of sediment – I was swimming in a cloud of dirt. My goal lay about 50 metres across and up the canal at a place where it was joined by a small stream. The stream led to a spring and, presumably, to the manatees. I began to swim. It was a bit eerie swimming along in the dim light of pre-dawn, with steam rising around me, and underwater visibility of about a dozen centimetres. I kept looking into the water to see if I could see the bottom, but I could not. Who knows how deep it was. Probably only about two metres. It might as well have been 1,000.

Suddenly, something bumped me, and I jumped. I put my face mask in the water and saw nothing. I felt around with my feet while treading water. What was it? I didn't know, but it was gone. An alligator? No, they are hibernating at this time of the year, I promised myself. A manatee? Let's hope so. I continued on.

I was drawing closer to the stream, constantly checking for alligators under water, but seeing nothing further away than my hands and camera. I had convinced myself that it was a manatee, but the possibility of an alligator still kept me in a state of alert. Just the day before a woman had been telling me that she had to shoot an alligator on her back dock the previous summer because it ate her dog! I didn't ask how big the dog was.

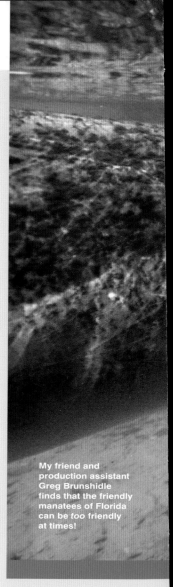

My friend and production assistant Greg Brunshidle finds that the friendly manatees of Florida can be *too* friendly at times!

Manatees can live in both salt water and fresh water

This manatee was digging through the sand looking for nutritious roots to eat. When I showed up with the camera, it found me more interesting.

This close-up of a manatee's head shows its short whiskers and tiny eyes. Note the closed nostrils.

Something bumped me again. I quickly jammed my head into the water to see just the slightest outline of something swimming away. There was no mistake about what it was. I'd know that big, flat pancake tail anywhere. Before I even got my head out of the water again, another manatee bumped me. She swam right up alongside of me and brushed her broad, algae-encrusted back against me. Was she having a little scratch? Saying hello? She was certainly not afraid of me.

I looked up to get a bearing, as I had stopped swimming while I watched the manatee and had lost my sense of direction. The stream was only a few metres away. I kicked faster.

As I got closer to the place where the small stream joined the canal, the water became clearer and clearer. I looked into the water and all around me there were manatees. The water was only two metres deep, and dozing on the bottom were manatees as far as I could see, which at that point was only about six metres in each direction. But I could count over 15 of them. Most were fast asleep, totally unaware of my presence. If I woke them up, would they be terrified of an intruder among them? Would they swim away as fast as they could? I thought they might, so I swam slowly and quietly over them,

Left: A severely damaged tail illustrates the problem manatees have sharing the waterways with speeding boats. A boat propeller cut this animal's tail in half. This manatee was lucky because it survived and appeared to be in good health.

being careful not to splash.

I headed up the small stream into the spring to find visibility easily exceeding 30 metres. The water was blue and crystal clear. I saw the hole about a metre across where the warm water comes out of the ground. I held my breath and swam down to the spring, feeling the rush of warm water past my face, and pondered the origins of the torrent. How far had this water travelled in order to emerge here? How long had the spring been producing this water? Without springs like this, manatees would never inhabit this part of the world, as they would never survive the winter. Like a watering hole in the African desert, this spring creates a refuge for manatees as an oasis of warmth in a chilly habitat.

As my breath-holding capability began to wane, I headed back towards the surface. Glancing skyward during my ascent, I saw a stunning sight: a manatee heading across the expanse of clear water directly towards me. The animal was a little bit curious, and not afraid at all. Here in the Crystal River area of Florida, manatees are accustomed to interacting with people. Some merely tolerate swimmers and snorkelers, but some actually seek out interactions with people, who gently scratch their backs and rub their tummies.

Later, I met a local man, living right next to the spring, who would go out in the morning and give the manatees a scrub with a big brush. They literally pushed and shoved to get their turn having a back scratch. It must feel really good to get all that algae off.

Average mature manatees are three metres long and weigh in the neighbourhood of 550 kilogrammes. However, some females may reach 4.5 metres and over 1,300 kilogrammes. My first experience in the water with a fully-grown manatee was surprising because I didn't really expect them to be so large. But despite their size, manatees are incredibly gentle. They have no natural predators and no need to be aggressive.

Yet, manatees face many challenges to survive in the wild – all of them caused by man. Because they are slow-moving and must surface to breathe in congested waterways filled with fast-moving boats, they are frequently hit by boats and propellers. In fact, about 85 per cent of the manatees in Florida show scars caused by boat propellers. Many animals are tracked and photo-identified by researchers using their unique tell-tale boat propeller scars. If this isn't bad enough, approximately 130 manatees die each year in Florida from collision with boats and laceration by the deadly propellers. Because the population of manatees in Florida is currently estimated at less than 3,000 animals, 130 deaths a year represents almost five per cent of the population – a significant and serious threat to their very existence. For the past two decades, manatee birth rates have just about matched the death rate, meaning that they are barely clinging to survival.

To reduce this terrible slaughter, many manatee refuges in Florida near warm water springs are

Above: While its mother sleeps, her calf suckles. The nipple is located in the 'armpit' behind the flipper, the same location as in elephants, which are the closest relatives of manatees.

Right: The springs are magical in the early morning, when the manatees can be photographed in clear water with a glass-smooth surface.

Above: In the Homosassa river of Florida, a large manatee approaches me cautiously, inching her way along the sandy bottom on her flippers.

Below: Many encounters with manatees occur in water so shallow that I can stand up, as on this morning in Crystal River.

either off limits to boat traffic, or have been posted with a speed limit. Although this does not guarantee the safety of manatees, it at least gives them a chance to get out of the way of oncoming boats. Manatees are also in a losing battle with man over habitat. As more and more of Florida gives way to development, they have fewer and fewer places to live and to find food. Mangrove habitats are being filled in and turned into canals lined with seawalls and houses.

Until the mid-1700s, there were huge manatees called Stellar's Sea Cows in the Bering Sea. Discovered in 1741, the Stellar's Sea Cow was hunted so heavily for its meat and hides that it became extinct. It was the largest Sirenian in recent history, very closely related to the still-living Sirenians. However, unlike the other known Sirenians, Stellar's Sea Cow lived in cold, arctic waters. Their numbers were so low and their existence so precariously balanced that it had taken humans only 27 years to kill every last one of them.

All manatees are believed to have evolved from a four-footed, plant-eating land mammal more than 60 million years ago. Although they look much like whales, blood sampling has shown that they are actually more closely related to elephants than to either whales or seals. Close examination of the toenails and rough skin of the manatee seems to support this evidence, as both show remarkable resemblance to those of elephants. Recent research has shown that the manatee and elephant share some unique anatomy in the inner ear. The evolutionary relationship of manatees to land animals is perhaps most obvious in the flippers, which still retain the finger bones of distant ancestors, even though the fingers themselves have long since been lost in order to form a flat paddle shape.

The manatee is a simple and docile grazer. It is the only completely herbivorous marine mammal in the entire world. In the wild, manatees will spend six to eight hours per day feeding, and may consume between about 30 and 90 kilogrammes of vegetation, or roughly ten per cent of their body weight. The nutritious roots of water plants, especially the water hyacinth, are a manatee favourite. Since this proliferating water weed is a nuisance to people, weed chomping manatees are natural weed-control agents.

During my first trip to swim with manatees, I had immersed myself in their world (literally) and had discovered something about myself, as well as the manatees. I found that I really cared about these animals, and they really are struggling to survive. This wasn't just some advertisement in a magazine for a fight to protect another endangered species – this was the real thing. The endangered species was made up of real, living, breathing animals, that I met and cared about. I became very alarmed. Three thousand are all that remain.

The Marine Mammal Protection Act of 1972 and the Endangered Species Act of 1973 were the first steps towards protection of the manatee in the United States. These laws make it illegal to harm, harass or kill any marine mammal, including manatees.

The manatee is the only completely herbivorous marine mammal in the entire world

However, these laws are not sufficient to protect the manatee from accidents with boats, loss of habitat and the other hazards they face. In 1978, the Florida Manatee Sanctuary Act was passed, making the entire state of Florida an official sanctuary. In addition, many local environmental organizations are helping the cause by raising funds to provide medical assistance to injured animals and by increasing public awareness of the plight of the manatee.

Perhaps one of the most impressive of manatee preservation programmes has come about almost by accident. Many manatees have begun to accumulate near power plants. These use bay water as coolant. Once released back into the bay, the water is unchanged except for a slightly higher temperature. Manatees use these artificially-warmed water sources in the same way that they use the springs: they congregate near them for the winter.

To help the manatees, many power companies have provided for the animals by giving them a source of fresh water to drink, and prohibiting boat traffic within the manatee zone. In addition, some of the companies have even set up manatee watching platforms for manatee enthusiasts, donating the proceeds to other preservation efforts.

Some critics argue that the manatees are coming to rely too much upon people for their survival. What if the power plant shut down in the middle of the winter and the warm water went away? What would the manatees do? In 1977 a partial shutdown of a plant on Florida's east coast is believed to have led to the death of 38 manatees. Now, many power companies have dug deep wells so that if the plant goes off line, warm water from deep within the earth can be pumped up to warm the animals.

There comes a time when people must decide how far they will go in their domination of the environment. We alone now hold the fate of the manatee in our hands. We can save them through simple management of our resources. We need to leave the manatees a portion of the world for themselves. Let us hope that we can find it within our hearts to leave some of the Earth to these gentle West Indian manatees, so that we may enjoy their company for years to come, and so that they do not suffer the same fate as Stellar's Sea Cow.

Above: A manatee feeding on one of its favourite foods – hydrilla. This weed can easily clog canals, but manatees can help by eating over 50 kg of it in a single day.

Far left: A manatee in the Homosassa River is reaching out of the water to feed on delicious overhanging plants. Manatees aren't called sea cows for nothing – they eat a lot of plants and aren't that choosy.

Left: An extremely plump manatee in silhouette in the Homosassa River.

Left: The large dome port on my camera lens fascinates the manatees because they see themselves reflected in it. I often find myself having a hard time backing away far enough to get pictures.

SEALS AND SEA LIONS

A pair of Galapagos sea lions (*Zalophus californianus wollebaeki*), playing in the shallows. These playful animals often interact with divers. They are actually the same species as the California sea lion, but because of their geographic separation, have been given their own sub-species.

Top: Harbor seals (*Phoca vitulina*) sunning themselves on the rocks in San Diego.
Harbor seals often haul out of the water to warm up and rest at low tide, then go back to hunt at high tide.

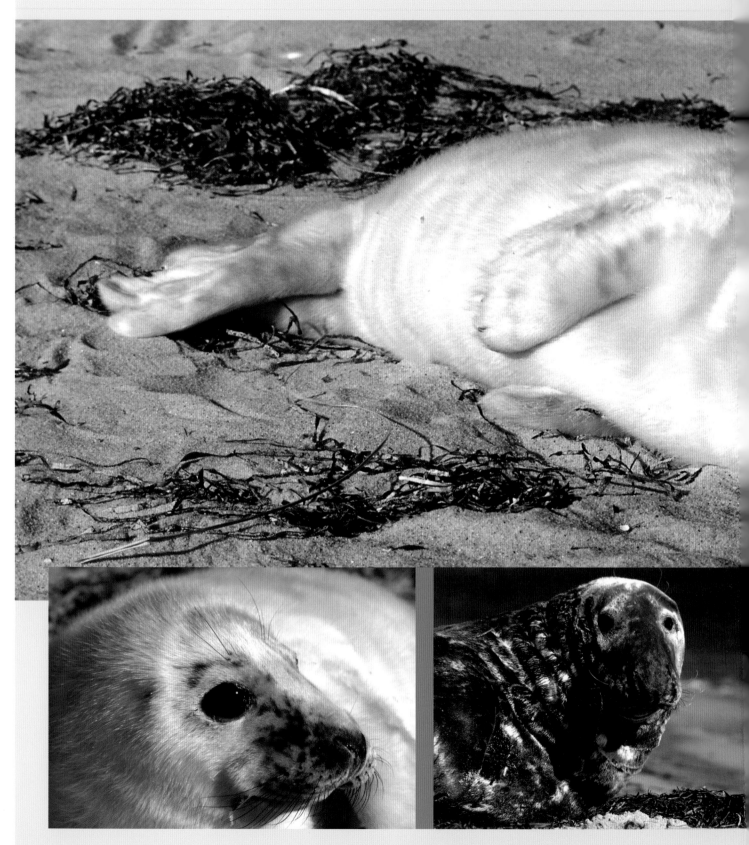

The seal noticed my bright blue Force Fins and came over to get a better look. The seal just loved the fins. He kept pulling on them and smelling them

Interacting with seals and sea lions is one of the most incredible experiences you can have underwater. They act like rumbustious underwater puppy dogs and often have that same curiosity about divers that you might expect from a dog, if only it could dive. They jet around in circles then quickly stop in front of you and bark. You can see the bubbles and hear the sound. Then they speed away looking for something more entertaining than a human. I have been fortunate to swim with seals and sea lions worldwide, from the coasts of Maine and California to the reefs of the Galapagos and Hawaii.

Like so many underwater experiences, my first interaction with seals is the most memorable. I heard that a dive operator in the Bar Harbor region of Maine had been diving with seals long enough for the seals to become accustomed to divers. In some parts of the world, seals are more friendly than others, probably due to increased exposure to people. In New England, seals do not have much human contact and consequently tend to be wary of them. Hearing of this opportunity to dive with the seals in Maine, some friends and I packed our gear and headed north for a week. I was working on a television film about the North Atlantic and I desperately needed to get some seal footage.

Top: A young Gray seal investigates the author's fin in the waters of Maine, USA.

Above: This Gray seal pup, resting on a breeding beach in February, is about a week old. The outside temperature is below zero. The seal is waiting for its mother to return from feeding so it can suckle. Gray seals go from birth to weaning in three weeks, so they drink a lot of milk, and the milk from the Gray seal is up to 60 per cent fat, the richest in the world. The pup will put on about 1 kg a day from its mother's milk.

Far left: A newborn Gray seal pup (*Halichoerus grypus*) has a coat of long white fur, which it keeps for about three weeks. After that, the pup moults to a shorter fur designed for swimming. The young pup needs the long fur because Gray seals are born in the middle of winter.

Left: A bull Gray seal showing the colouration of an adult. The males grow to over 300 kg in weight and 3 metres long.

After the boat ride out, we arrived at the island. My diving buddies and I dropped from the boat into 12 metres of water and swam together towards the small group of seals on the shore. We settled down in about 4.5 metres of water and waited and waited and waited. We spent two days sitting there and saw nothing, except each other and some seaweed. We knew the seals were all around us, but they would not come close. On the third day, after what seemed like an eternity, a large Gray seal (*Halichoerus grypus*) finally appeared. It moved towards us cautiously. My friend Phil held out his hand. The seal took it into its mouth and began to gnaw on it gently. Phil had tremendously thick neoprene gloves on, as we all did, because of the freezing water. The seal could easily have bitten right through them. Yet its body language never implied a threat. When people see the footage of the incident they wonder what we were thinking, but honestly, at the time, it seemed no more dangerous than playing with a dog. After a few minutes of playing with Phil, the seal noticed my bright blue Force Fins and came over to get a better look. The seal just loved the fins. He kept pulling on them and smelling them. I passed the video camera to Phil and let him shoot the action from a better perspective. It was a wonderful day, one I will never forget. What an amazing first encounter with a seal!

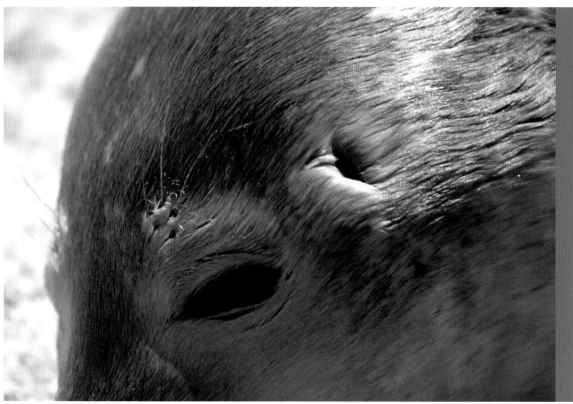

The ear opening of a Harbor seal. This is a *True seal*, having no external ear flaps. It can close its ears to keep water out when diving.

A juvenile Hawaiian Monk seal (*Monachus schauinslandi*) one of the rarest seals in the world, resting on the beach at Midway Atoll in the baking sun.

Above: A juvenile Harbor seal resting in a tide pool in Maine, USA. Its whiskers are thought to play a role in hunting for food at close range.

Right: This Harbor seal pup in San Diego is only an hour or so old. It still has the umbilical cord attached and folds in its skin from the womb.

Seals and sea lions belong to the order *Pinnipedia*, which means 'wing-footed'. This is a reference to the feet which have evolved into flippers. There are three families of pinnipeds: the Eared or Fur seals (*Otariidae*, which includes the group commonly called sea lions), the true seals (*Phocidae*), and the walrus (*Odobenidae*, of which there is only one species in the world). The basic difference between Eared seals and True seals is in the basic body form and how it is used in swimming and walking. Eared seals have muscular front flippers that can be used to support the weight of the animal's upper body and lift the head off the ground. These front flippers provide the swimming power, while the back flippers act like rudders to steer. Additionally, Eared seals can rotate their rear flippers to point forward, to help them walk on land. They also have external ear flaps, hence their name.

True seals cannot lift their bodies from the ground or rotate their rear flippers forward, and must move on land with an awkward belly crawl. Once in the water, however, True seals are extremely quick, using their rear flippers for locomotion, not the front flippers. True seals, for example, the Harbor seal, have small ear openings but no ear flaps.

A group of Harbor seals has taken over a popular swimming beach in San Diego, California.

Left: A mother nurses a Galapagos sea lion pup.

They may be awkward on land, but in the water seals swim as gracefully as eagles soaring in the sky

Below: A Galapagos sea lion playing in the waters of the southern Galapagos.

Bottom: A sleeping Galapagos sea lion.

While whales and dolphins have adopted an entirely marine life, pinnipeds maintain a strong tie with land. They come ashore to rest and bask in the sun. Females, called cows, give birth on shore and nurse their pups there. They enter the water to hunt, feed and play. Some species of seal and sea lion actually take naps underwater, but usually not for long. Everything about pinnipeds is geared towards their ability to survive in the water. They may be awkward on land, but in the water seals swim as gracefully as eagles soaring in the sky. Like other mammals, seals and sea lions have a layer of blubber under the skin, and hair on the body. The hair has many oil glands to increase insulation. During a dive, the circulation to most of the body, except the brain and vital internal organs, is severely restricted. The heartbeat slows to as low as 1/10th the normal surface rate and the body temperature falls to conserve oxygen. All of this allows the seal to stay submerged longer. While submerged, most pinnipeds can swim at about 12 kilometres per hour.

Above: Mother and pup Galapagos sea lions.

A Galapagos sea lion is hunting for shellfish on the bottom.

Above: Years of protection mean that sea lions in the Galapagos are accustomed to people and go back to sleep even with humans around. This close-up shows the ear flaps that Eared seals like sea lions have.

Seals and sea lions can see well in the ocean, having eyes designed to focus underwater, but they have somewhat limited vision on land. Yet vision is apparently not essential for survival. Many blind seals and sea lions have been reported in perfect health. Pinnipeds possess acute hearing both in water and on land. They can even close their ear openings and nostrils to keep water out during a dive. The olfactory sense of seals and sea lions operates in both air and water. To sense vibration and touch, seals and sea lions have whiskers called *vibrissae*, which are like those of a dog or a cat. They are thought to play a role in food capture at short range by detecting the vibrations of their prey.

The most playful pinnipeds I have ever

Sea lions move quickly and show amazing flexibility. Their graceful movements are hard to capture in still images but this illustration gives an idea.

Below left: A Galapagos sea lion blowing bubbles. Sea lions often remind me of young children, inventing clever ways to entertain themselves.

Below: A big bull Galapagos sea lion showing how sea lions, unlike True seals, can stand up on their front flippers to walk.

encountered underwater are the sea lions in the Galapagos Islands. They are not afraid of people at all – apparently aware of their protected status. On the beach, they allow people to walk right up to them and take pictures, but they tend to keep to themselves. In the water though, it's a different story. Here they cavort like puppies, swimming back and forth and up and down in front of divers as if to show off how superior their water skills really are. They sneak up behind divers and pull their fins, they bark in your face to establish who is boss, and their favourite trick is to zoom by so fast that in pictures they end up looking like a blur. My wife Christine loves to snorkel with the sea lions in the Galapagos and has to be dragged from the water at the end of the day after hours of exhausting fun.

In many places, pinnipeds are now protected. However, that was not always the case. In August 1494, Columbus landed on an island somewhere south of Haiti and killed eight 'sea wolves' which were sleeping on the sand. And so began the destruction of the West Indian Monk seal (*Monachus tropicalis*). From the 1700's to the 1900's, the West Indian Monk seal was slaughtered for its meagre fat. Unlike most other marine mammals which thrive in cooler areas, the warm habitat of the West Indian Monk seal meant that it had little blubber from which to render oil. But it was free for the taking and relatively abundant, and there were colonies of the animals all around the Caribbean. We can only infer their former range of habitats today from all the different islands and atolls named 'seal island' or 'Lobos Cay' (Lobos is Spanish for wolf). But we'll never know how many West Indian Monk seals once lived. We will never know what they ate, or how they mated. We will never get to see them give birth to a new pup, or swim through the clear waters of the shallows, or investigate a diver's camera, because they're all gone.

Humans killed *every single* Monk seal in the Caribbean. When you think about it, that's quite an achievement. After all, killing every single one of something – anything – is fairly difficult. But humans managed to do it. We will never know what the West Indian Monk seal might have taught us about the sea, about mammals, about science, or about ourselves. The Caribbean Monk seal was the most recent marine mammal extinction in history, with the last living specimens seen in the 1950s. Today, the Hawaiian Monk seal and Mediterranean Monk seal are clinging to survival. Scientists believe that fewer than 500 Mediterranean Monk seals still survive, and that there are fewer than 1,000 Hawaiian Monk seals left. This makes them among the most endangered animals on Earth.

Right: A Hawaiian Monk seal hunting for fish in the waters around Midway Atoll.

Far right: This Galapagos sea lion stopped in front of my camera, looked right at me and barked, leaving a little trail of bubbles.

Below: A Gray seal pup on a beach in Canada.

I can't help but adore their puppy dog whiskers and eyes

Several years ago I visited Midway Atoll on a magazine assignment during the brief time the island was open to visitors. There I saw my first Hawaiian Monk seal in the wild. It was lounging on a beach taking a nap. I crouched behind a log more than a hundred yards away with a monstrous telephoto lens to photograph the animal without disturbing it. They are not only easily spooked, but are so rare and endangered that every single animal is afforded as much protection as possible. Entire sections of Midway Atoll were off limits because the Monk seals would haul out of the water to sleep in those areas. It's unclear whether this species will survive, so it needs all the help it can get. Diving at Kauaii Island, Christine and I came upon a Hawaiian Monk seal asleep on the sea bottom. It awoke with a start as we came around a pile of rocks and I'm not sure who was more surprised! That is the only time I have seen one underwater.

Fortunately, unlike the Monk seals, most species of pinnipeds are thriving. In California, sea lion populations have rebounded from overhunting so well that they are now taking over the waterfront in some places. In San Francisco they have become almost a nuisance by congregating in large numbers on the docks. Even so, I can't help but adore their puppy dog whiskers and eyes, and remember my first underwater encounter with these graceful animals those years ago.

SEA TURTLES

Left: Newborn Green sea turtle hatchlings (*Chelonia mydas*) run down the sand to the water at dawn. Survival depends on getting from the beach to the open sea as quickly as possible.

Below: A Green sea turtle rising for a breath of air in the waters of Hawaii. Although they live most of their lives in the water, these animals are reptiles and must breathe air at the surface.

While fish have been very successful at populating the oceans, and mammals have adapted to the sea in many forms, reptiles have only a handful of oceanic representatives. A few species of snake have evolved into ocean inhabitants. One type of lizard and some crocodiles regularly hunt in the sea for food. But sea turtles are the only group of reptiles to spend most of their lives in the water. They maintain their ties with land to lay eggs, but otherwise they have become full-time ocean residents. Because the water supports their bodies, sea turtles can attain sizes far greater than they could if they lived solely on land. One of the most common 'big animals' that divers encounter on tropical reefs, sea turtles are also often a diver's first experience of large marine animals.

One of the most amazing turtle sanctuaries on Earth is on the tiny Malaysian island of Sipadan. The island is so small that you can walk all the way round it on the beach in about half an hour. In 1984 Jacques Cousteau visited this island with his research ship the Calypso and produced a documentary about the sea turtles and incredible marine ecosystem. The film prompted divers from all over the world to venture to Sipadan and explore it for themselves.

A company called Borneo Divers developed a diving resort on the island, and divers flocked there. It soon became famous as one of the best places in the world to see sea turtles, not just swimming around on the reefs, but nesting at night on the beach. Every night, all year long, turtles come ashore to dig their nests, bury their eggs, and return to the ocean. As a result, nests of eggs hatch nearly every night and hundreds of the hatchlings scurry to the sea to start the cycle again.

Top: A Green sea turtle sunning itself on the beach in Hawaii. There are very few places in the world where sea turtles, which are primarily ocean creatures, actually come out of the ocean to rest. I have only seen this happen in Hawaii.

Above: Once they reach the water, the baby sea turtles swim out to sea to escape predators on the reef. They will not return to the reef for several years.

Left and far left: On a beach in Malaysia, baby sea turtles all hatch from their nest in the sand at the same time and rush down the beach as a group in an attempt to escape predators.

My friend Alice Kline has encountered a Loggerhead sea turtle (*Caretta caretta*) on a shipwreck in the Bahamas.

Right: Another Loggerhead sea turtle is taking a nap under some wreckage of the same ship. Sea turtles sleep quite soundly while holding their breath for several hours.

Below right: A Green sea turtle searching the reef for food in the waters of Malaysia. Adult Green turtles feed almost exclusively on marine plants.

But it wasn't always this way. Collecting turtle eggs has been prevalent on Sipadan for years, with collectors digging up the nests each night and selling the eggs in the marketplace. Interestingly, sea turtle egg collection and trafficking are illegal in Malaysia, but Sipadan is a special egg collecting 'law-free zone' because of an old favour.

The story goes that the wife of the Sultan of Sulu was attacked by pirates near Sipadan in the 1800's, but the people of the region rescued her. To express his gratefulness, the Sultan gave a few families in the area a special permit to take turtle eggs on Sipadan; a permit which is still considered legally binding today. But only the few descendants of those people are allowed to collect the eggs. In an effort to protect this productive hatchery, some of the dive operators on Sipadan decided to try to stop the egg collecting. Borneo Divers and two of the other resorts on the island pooled their resources to pay off the collectors. They thought that paying these descendants not to take the eggs would keep them safe.

For ten years, the diving shops on Sipadan paid the collectors about $50,000 a year not to collect eggs. Recently, the Malaysian government closed Sipadan to dive resorts because there were too many on the island and the impact of all their septic systems was degrading the marine ecosystem. The resorts relocated to nearby islands. Sipadan is now a National Park, protected by a small resident military force. Divers can still scuba dive there, but they can no longer stay on the island or go ashore at night. This gives the turtle population even more protection, not just from egg poachers but from well-intentioned human interference.

In 2007 I was working on a film about coral reefs and wanted to shoot a sequence featuring sea turtles. I hoped to take my film crew to Sipadan, as I would be able to film every aspect of the behaviour of the turtles, from feeding to mating, to sleeping. Unfortunately, the government denied my request to film nesting turtles at night on the beach. Instead, they suggested I film at another island called Selingan, not far away, where they have staff studying the nesting turtles every night.

On any given night during the high season for egg-laying, from September to November, more than 20 turtles may crawl up the beach on Selingan, each laying more than 100 eggs. Because there are more sea turtles than space for nests, the full-time turtle officers carefully monitor each nesting turtle and mark the location of the nest. Once the female has finished laying her eggs and gone back to the ocean, the officers dig up the eggs and relocate them to a nursery further from the beach. Each nest in the nursery is dug to the same depth that the mother sea turtle dug, and then the nest is marked with the date and surrounded with a fence against predators. About two months later the baby turtles are due to hatch, and the nests are closely watched by the officers. At the first sign of movement, they help dig out the baby turtles and take them to the water's edge, releasing them into the ocean without land predators to attack them.

When a nest of eggs hatches naturally, the baby turtles must emerge from the sand all at once and dash down the beach as quickly as possible to reach the water. They have to run for their lives before they are gobbled up by lizards, crabs, birds, feral cats, and a host of other predators. Once they make it to the water, they must cross the shallows and then the reef, where they are food for barracuda, sharks, diving birds and other animals.

Above: A baby Green sea turtle heading offshore as fast as it can swim. This turtle will not come back near a reef until it is several years old and about the size of a dinner plate. At that point, only large sharks will be able to eat it.

Right: A Green sea turtle in the waters of Hawaii. Although Green turtles often have algae on their shells, making them appear green, they get their name from the greenish tint of the fat in their tissue. The colour comes from their entirely herbivorous diet.

Inset right: This baby Green sea turtle is only a few minutes old, but may live over 100 years.

Baby turtles must dash down the beach quickly to reach the water, before they are gobbled up by lizards, crabs, birds, feral cats, and a host of other predators. Once they make it to the water, they must cross the shallows and then the reef, where they are food for barracuda, sharks, diving birds and other animals

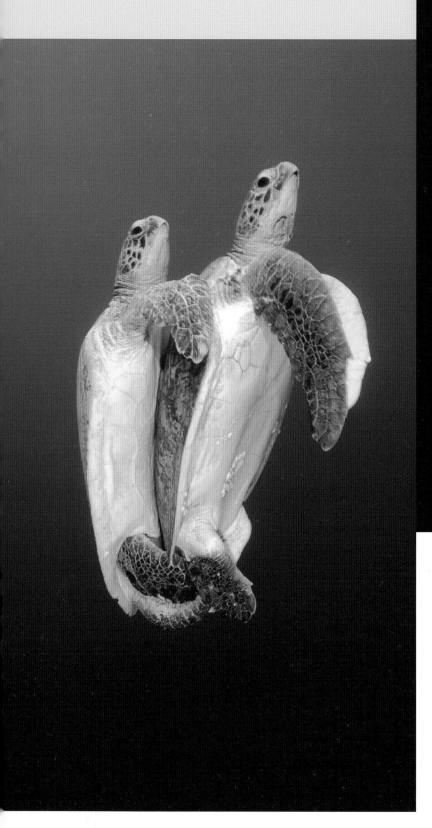

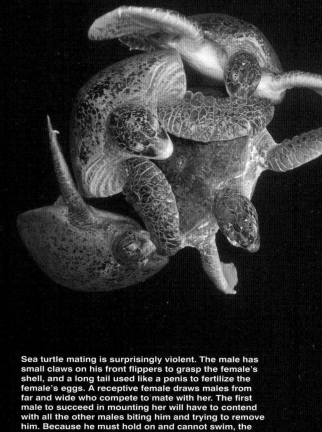

Sea turtle mating is surprisingly violent. The male has small claws on his front flippers to grasp the female's shell, and a long tail used like a penis to fertilize the female's eggs. A receptive female draws males from far and wide who compete to mate with her. The first male to succeed in mounting her will have to contend with all the other males biting him and trying to remove him. Because he must hold on and cannot swim, the female must swim – and rise to breathe – for both of them. Sometimes the female can practically drown. The process may go on for several hours.

The hatchlings head for the open ocean. They are not safe on the reef. As air-breathing reptiles, they must surface to breathe, and cannot hide in the reef all the time. The reef is a dangerous place for a baby sea turtle. So they swim far offshore, hiding in mats of floating seaweed where grow larger feeding on jellyfish. It's no wonder that typically only one hatchling out of 100 survives to adulthood.

Once the sea turtle reaches the size of a dinner plate, it is too large to be a meal for

anything but the larger sharks, and heads back to the reef to live. It will be a few more years before it will reach sexual maturity. Scientists suspect that female turtles always return to the beach of their birth to lay their eggs. Nobody is quite sure how they figure out how to get to that beach, how they remember it, or how they know when they are in the right place. It could be a memory of the smell, a magnetic bearing they can somehow sense, or something else. Sea turtles spend years in the open ocean, but when it's time to mate and lay eggs, they return to the area where they were born.

Sea turtle mating is a violent and difficult undertaking for both male and female. A male must chase down a female, then grab onto her shell and ride her. He has tiny claw-like nails on his front flippers to clasp the front of the female's shell. Then he uses his long tail to wrap around underneath her shell and enter her cloaca. The tail is used like a penis, which is why male sea turtles have much longer tails than females.

She drops about 100 soft, squishy eggs the size of ping pong balls into the nest, in about ten minutes

Right and below right: A large female Green turtle nesting in Malaysia. She has dug a hole about a metre deep with her rear flippers and is dropping about 100 eggs into the hole. After she covers them up and leaves, they will take about two months to hatch.

Below: A Black sea turtle (*Chelonia agassizi*) in the waters of the Galapagos is so closely related to the Green turtle that many scientists believe it is the same species, even though the Black turtle has a unique appearance. It only inhabits the tropical Eastern Pacific Ocean.

Once the male has grabbed on, the female must swim for both of them, including rising to breathe. She quickly becomes exhausted. Meanwhile, other males in the area come to join the action and try to dislodge the male from his female. They bite his flippers, stick their heads between the mating pair, blow bubbles beneath them, and try everything they can to get the mating male off the female. This may go on for several hours. Even though the male may have finished the task, he still stays on the female a while longer to be sure nobody else gets a shot at fertilizing her eggs.

Once the act of mating is completed, the hard work for the female has only just begun. She waits until night to deposit the eggs in a nest on the beach. After sunset she swims into shallow water and makes her way out of the water and up the sand. When turtles are coming ashore to nest, they are very sensitive to light and sound. Anything out of the ordinary will frighten them and send them scurrying back into the water. These animals are extremely ungainly and vulnerable on land. They can swim as gracefully as dolphins in the sea, but the slow crawl up the beach is exhausting and frightening for a sea turtle. Once a suitable place has been found, the

female begins digging a pit around her body. Next she digs an egg chamber with her rear flippers. She does this entirely by feel because she can't see behind her while she is digging. She digs a narrow hole around a metre deep, taking one scoop at a time out of the sand with her rear flippers, which are curled into a spoon-like shape.

Once she starts laying eggs into the hole, she will not stop. Even lights in her face and a strobe from a flash unit will not deter her from her mission – she is now fully committed. She drops about 100 soft, squishy eggs the size of ping pong balls into the nest, over the course of about ten minutes. Then she gently covers over the hole, and flings sand around to disguise the exact location of the nest, providing further protection from predators. Once she is satisfied that the eggs are safe, she laboriously crawls – exhausted and overheated – back to the ocean. She stops every few seconds to catch her breath. You can tell by the sound of her laboured breathing that she feels like someone who has just run a marathon. The whole process of laying the eggs takes several hours and when she has finished, she heads back to the reef and takes a well-deserved nap!

In the 1600's and 1700's, shipping captains used the Cayman Islands in the Caribbean as regular stops because of their large numbers of Green turtles. The turtles served as an abundant and free source of meat on their voyages. After a while, people began living on the Caymans, and they too hunted the turtles for food and export. By the 1800's, the turtles had become very scarce indeed. Today, sea turtles are protected in the waters of the Cayman Islands. Hunting wild sea turtles is now of course illegal, but to this day, their meat is still served in the Caymans – one of the few remaining places where people regularly eat them. The turtles come from a farm started in 1968 on Grand Cayman. A small percentage of the farmed turtles are released to help stock up the wild population, while the rest are kept for food and shell products. Between 1980 and 2006, the farm released almost 31,000 sea turtles into the waters around

Above: A Black sea turtle hatchling in the Galapagos seen compared to a hand. It's hard to believe that this turtle can grow to more than 200 kg.

Right: Green sea turtles at the Cayman Turtle Farm in Grand Cayman. Because sea turtles are a traditional delicacy in the Cayman Islands, they are farmed for meat. The farm also releases a small percentage of the turtles annually.

Far right: A female Hawksbill sea turtle (*Eretmochelys imbricata*) in the waters of the Cayman Islands. Male and female sea turtles are easy to differentiate: males have extremely long tails and females have short ones.

the Cayman Islands. The wild sea turtle population has increased dramatically, so it must be working. Whether or not the farmed turtles go on to lead a normal life after they are released is a mystery. Some observers suspect that they may lack some survival instincts and might not be able to find their nesting beaches again. Given the long lifespan of turtles, it may be a while before we know how the captive-release turtles are faring in the wild.

Top: A Hawksbill sea turtle in the waters of Honduras in the Caribbean.

Above: It is thought that Green sea turtles migrate back to the beach of their birth to lay their eggs and at least one Green turtle was tracked swimming over 2,600 km!

Right: A Green sea turtle taking a breath.

Above left: A Green sea turtle in Hawaii feeding on algae in the shallows. Sea turtles rarely come into water this shallow as they are vulnerable, but in Hawaii they do it all the time.

Above: In an underwater cave at Sipadan Island, the remains of a Green sea turtle prove that turtles *can* drown. This turtle went so far into the cave that it couldn't find its way back out.

Left: A Green sea turtle on a reef at Sipadan Island, Malaysia.

Turtles have faced many obstacles to their survival, almost all of which have been created by people. Millions of years ago, before humans existed, turtles were crawling up the beach, laying their eggs and generally carrying on exactly the way they do now. They have changed very little since then. Along comes *Homo sapiens*, and all bets are off. We eat their eggs, we kill them for meat, we catch them by accident in gill nets where they drown, and we kill them for their shells. The list goes on. Such ancient animals, with their slow reproductive rate, are no match for our ability to kill them. Turtle populations are declining in most parts of the world. Beaches in central America that used to have thousands of turtles laying eggs on them now have only tens, or none. Islands whose waters once teemed with turtles are stripped bare of them. On all but a few Caribbean islands, sea turtles are an uncommon sight. But there is hope. Alerted to the danger, people have begun to make changes in the way sea turtles are treated. Shrimp fishermen in the Gulf of Mexico, who used to kill a lot of them accidentally in their trawl nets, are now required to use a so-called Turtle Excluder Device on their equipment. This is a special kind of hatch door in the net which ejects large animals like turtles but doesn't allow smaller animals, like shrimp, to escape. They do work – not 100 per cent of the time – but well enough to save the lives of thousands of turtles a year.

Right: A Hawksbill sea turtle resting under a coral overhang in the waters of Dominica in the Caribbean. The Hawksbill is at home on the reef since it eats reef sponges.

These ancient mariners who have bridged the worlds of land and sea for hundreds of millions of years are not yet out of danger

Sea turtles are now protected in the United States and in almost all of the Caribbean. It is completely illegal to harm a sea turtle. It is even illegal to import sea turtle products into the U.S., even if they were bought legally in another country. For example, it is legal to buy shell products from the turtle farm in the Cayman Islands, but it is illegal to bring them back to the U.S.

A new awareness of the plight of sea turtles, combined with efforts to protect their breeding beaches, stop egg collecting and stop turtle hunting, has made a tremendous difference. In many places, turtles are making a strong comeback. Not all species are recovering equally, but sea turtle conservation is definitely helping.

And the story of sea turtle conservation is one with a good outlook. It proves that with protection and effort, an endangered species *can* be saved and gives hope for the protection and recovery of other at-risk creatures. These ancient mariners who have bridged the worlds of land and sea for hundreds of millions of years are not yet out of danger, but in many areas they are recovering exceptionally well. With continued effort and diligence, sea turtles will be around to thrive for millions of years to come.

Left: Another turtle waiting its turn at the cleaning station.

Below: This Green sea turtle at Sipadan Island has three remoras on its shell. These fish have a sucker-cup to allow them to hold on to larger animals like turtles, sharks and dolphins for a free ride. They don't seem to bother the turtles.

ACKNOWLEDGEMENTS

A great many people have helped me with my underwater photography along the way. I owe a great debt of thanks to: my wife Christine for her encouragement, support and expert underwater modelling; my good friends Art Cohen, Tim Geers, Tom Krasuski, and Greg "Gator" Brunshidle at O.R.G.; David Evans and John Mitchell at Evans Mitchell Publishing; Darren Westlake; Caroline Smith; Peter and Gillian Varley; Bob Evans at Force Fin; Jean Brigham, Larry Ostendorf, Glenn Goodrich, and the outstanding people and products of Ikelite Underwater Systems; Julia Cichowski; Kerry and Linda Hurd; Pierre Seguin; Mark Tarczynski; Scott Matey; Nigel Campbell; Terri Hyde, Meredith Reynolds; Sherrie Floyd, Scott Krause, New England Aquarium; Tracy Beckett and Madeleine Carter, National Geographic Channel International; Peter Arnold; Sue Dabritz-Yuen, Seapics; Doug Perrine; Jeffrey Bird, Parrelli Optical; Inez Smith, Wayne Scott Smith and Andy Pickrell, Dolphin Dream Team; Glen Holmes and Jules Morton; Dave "Puumba" Fabian; Kurt Nose; Todd and Lynne Sisto; Chip Deutsch, Bob Bonde, Sirenia Project, U.S. Geological Survey; Betsy Dearth, Homosassa Springs State Wildlife Park; Cynthia Carrion, Philippines Department of Tourism; Gerry Voo, Borneo Divers; Sharon Pascal, Dominica Tourism; Fred Dion, Underwater Photo Tech; Kathy Simoneau; Charlie Donilon, Snappa Diving Charters; Dave Sinclair, Sea Ventures; Gerry Flagg; Ed "Lamper Yanker" Woods; Drew Bradley; Wilfrido Sánchez Arriaga; Bob Bosien; Dr. Mike Wilke; Al and Wendy Bozza; Rick Gaffney, Destination Midway; Stuart and Michelle Cove, Graham Cove, Stuart Cove Dive South Ocean; Rick and Cindy Allen; Renate Eichinger and Bobby Edwards, Atlantis Diving Charters; Ty Sawyer, Ann Louise Tuke, Connie Sue White, Carrie Garcia, Jennifer Collier Pileggi, Sport Diver Magazine; Reneé Duncan, Steve Mehan, Alert Diver Magazine; Cathryn Castle, Dive Training Magazine; John Eliot and Chris Scaptura, National Geographic Magazine; Holly Martel-Bourbon; Mary Brennan, Marcella Martinez Associates; Terry Evans and Pat Stoddard, Roatan Charters; Ken Knezick, Island Dreams Tours & Travel; Jim and Kisty Engel, Jim McClendon, Willy Waterhouse and Albert Stubbs, Utila Lodge, Honduras; Lene Petersen; Digna Dominguez and David Chinchilla, Honduras Institute of Tourism; TACA Airlines; David Gonzalez, America Central Corporation; Rebecca Rosen, Bozell Public Relations; Dr. Stephen Turnbull; Tony Medcraft, Exmouth Diving Centre; Chief Thomas Dutton, USCG; Bob Bowman, Dr. Steven Katona, The College of the Atlantic; Tim Cole, Stephanie Martin, Ann Zoidis, Allen Reitsch, Lisa Cuellar, Mount Desert Rock Whale and Sea Bird Research Station; Chris and Elaine Eaton, Harbor Divers, Maine; Stefan Arnold; Tracy Sundell, Nantucket Marine Department.

I would also like to thank the many researchers and biologists who gave freely of their time and knowledge. Without them, this book would never have existed. Although I have tried to have everything reviewed by experts in the field, any errors in this book are mine.

All photographs by Jonathan Bird except page 53 by Christine Bird

CONVERSION TABLES

This book was published using Metric weights and measurements. It is hoped that this will in no way spoil your enjoyment or distract from the informative text. However, this brief conversion table is offered to be helpful where metric figures occur. In most cases the conversions are to the nearest practical unit.

DISTANCE & SPEED

10 cm is equal to 4 inches
10 metres is equal to 33 feet
1 kilometre is equal to 0.6 miles
  thus
80 kilometres per hour
  is the equivalent of 50 miles per hour

AREA

100 square metres is equal to
  1,076 square feet
  (for most purposes simply multiple by 10)
10 square kilometres
  is equal to 3.86 square miles
  (again, use 4 as a practical figure)
100 hectares is equal to 247 acres
  is equal to 0.4 square miles

WEIGHTS

1 kilogramme is equal to 2.2 lbs
100 kilos is equal to 220 lbs

TEMPERATURES

A simple formula to convert from Celsius (centigrade) to Fahrenheit is to multiply by 1.8 and add 32
  thus
15° Celsius is equal to 59° Fahrenheit
25° Celsius is equal to 77° Fahrenheit

OTHER

Wild things...

TITLES

Wild Things...
The Great Apes
ISBN: 978-1-901268-31-7

Wild Things...
Gorillas
ISBN: 978-1-901268-35-5

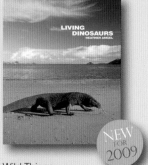

Wild Things...
Living Dinosaurs
ISBN: 978-1-901268-36-2

Other wildlife titles published by

 **Evans Mitchell Books**

www.embooks.co.uk

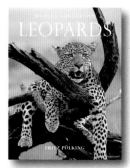

Wildlife Monographs
Cheetahs
ISBN: 978-1-901268-09-6

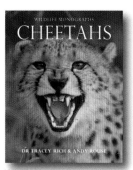

Wildlife Monographs
Elephants
ISBN: 978-1-901268-08-9

Wildlife Monographs
Giant Pandas
ISBN: 978-1-901268-13-3

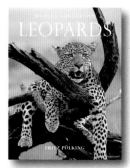

Wildlife Monographs
Loepards
ISBN: 978-1-901268-12-6

Wildlife Monographs
Sharks
ISBN: 978-1-901268-11-9

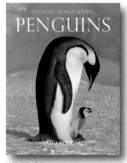

Wildlife Monographs
Penguins
ISBN: 978-1-901268-14-0

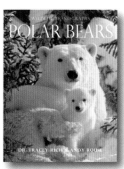

Wildlife Monographs
Polar Bears
ISBN: 978-1-901268-15-7

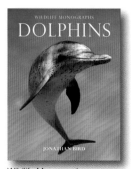

Wildlife Monographs
Dolphins
ISBN: 978-1-901268-17-1

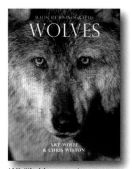

Wildlife Monographs
Wolves
ISBN: 978-1-901268-18-8

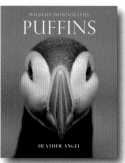

Wildlife Monographs
Puffins
ISBN: 978-1-901268-19-5

Wildlife Monographs
Monkeys of the Amazon
ISBN: 978-1-901268-10-2